WITHDRAWN

Praise for *In Great Company*

In Great Company explores the humanity of an organization and the importance of emotional connectedness. The book offers a set of frameworks and a plethora of practical examples and approaches that can help unleash the power of the people and extraordinary performance.

—**Hubert Joly,** Chairman and CEO, Best Buy

For nearly three decades, Louis Carter has been a visionary and pioneer in helping organizations achieve peak performance from their employees. Louis's process for *In Great Company* really works. I have been practicing this with him in my companies for over 15 years, creating wins for everyone—clients/customers, company, teams, individuals. The process develops the greatest culture, with the greatest people in place, and the greatest systems for collaboration, which is the best way to transform and generate real results.

—**Brian Fishel,** Chief Human Resources Officer, KeyBank

An incredibly important book that will change the way we lead and manage today. Carter distills the essence of what it takes to be a truly great leader—forge functional, respectful, generous relationships with those you lead and follow.

—**Frances Hesselbein,** Chairman, Frances Hesselbein Leadership Institute; Editor in Chief, *Leader to Leader* journal; Presidential Medal of Freedom Recipient

An invaluable toolkit for experienced and aspiring leaders alike! Recognizing people as central to success, Carter leverages his vast insight into corporate America to coach managers on how to build and leverage strong relationships to thrive and win in today's dynamic, changing world. His guidance through best practices checklists and immediate action steps gives every leader a place to start or improve leadership skills, build effective teams, continue to grow, and, ultimately, achieve positive results.

> —**Karen Dyson,** Lieutenant General, U.S. Army (retired); formerly, Military Deputy to the Assistant Secretary of the Army for Financial Management and Comptroller; currently, Board Director, USAA Federal Savings Bank and CALIBRE

Move over IQ and EQ—it's time to make room on the shelf for EC (emotional connectedness). In his new book, *In Great Company*, Louis Carter shares a rare combination of in-depth analysis and Monday-morning pragmatism to uncover the essential (and usually missing) ingredient of true organizational and leadership success: deep emotional connectedness.

> —**Paul L. Corona,** MBA, EdD, Clinical Associate Professor of Leadership; Director of full-time MBA Leadership Development, Kellogg School of Management at Northwestern University

I care deeply about becoming the best possible CEO and leader, which is why I have chosen to work with Louis on the principles and practices in this book, *In Great Company*, and I can say without doubt that they really work. His executive coaching on emotional connectedness has brought me great insights for my leadership at Springfield Clinic because it has helped me forge more emotionally connected relationships within my company, community, and patients—enrolling everyone as thought partners in my development and the betterment of the organization.

There is no more important task in healthcare than to care deeply about the development and highest quality of care within our clinic. Lou's coaching has helped me to do what is top of my mind as a CEO—developing and sustaining caring, respectful, collaborative relationships that have the very best outcome for our staff and patients. When you forge a bond that is respectful of patients and employees, you will always win.

—**Ray Williams**, CEO, Springfield Clinic

I have a passion and mission to do what is right for patients and help to save lives and reduce the suffering caused by hospital infections like staph, C. diff, MRSA, and VRE.

Louis's book *In Great Company* and his coaching and work around emotional connectedness have helped us further our mission.

After incorporating his methods for becoming a more emotionally connected leader, I have become more aware of the incredible possibilities with clients, employees, and prospects to forge respectful, values-driven, and deep collaborative relationships where everyone wins.

We are applying the new principles of emotional connectedness to our client relationships as well as internally, and we have already seen unexpected and impressive outcomes.

—**Morris Miller**, CEO, Xenex Disinfection Systems and cofounder, Rackspace

IN GREAT COMPANY

HOW TO SPARK
PEAK PERFORMANCE
BY CREATING AN
EMOTIONALLY CONNECTED
WORKPLACE

LOUIS CARTER

NEW YORK   CHICAGO   SAN FRANCISCO
ATHENS   LONDON   MADRID
MEXICO CITY   MILAN   NEW DELHI
SINGAPORE   SYDNEY   TORONTO

1 2 3 4 5 6 7 8 9   QVS   24 23 22 21 20 19

ISBN 978-1-260-14316-4
MHID   1-260-14316-3

e-ISBN 978-1-260-14317-1
e-MHID   1-260-14317-1

Library of Congress Cataloging-in-Publication Data

Names: Carter, Louis, author.
Title: In great company : how to spark peak performance by creating an
   emotionally connected workplace / Louis Carter.
Description: New York : McGraw-Hill, [2019]
Identifiers: LCCN 2018046215| ISBN 9781260143164 (alk. paper) | ISBN
   1260143163
Subjects: LCSH: Organizational behavior. | Emotional intelligence. | Employee
   motivation. | Corporate culture.
Classification: LCC HD58.7 .C353 2019 | DDC 658.3/14—dc23 LC record available
at https://lccn.loc.gov/2018046215

McGraw-Hill Education books are available at special quantity discounts to use as premiums and sales promotions or for use in corporate training programs. To contact a representative, please visit the Contact Us pages at www.mhprofessional.com.

*I dedicate this book to
all those in pursuit of a
better world of work.*

CONTENTS

FOREWORD

When Louis told me his new book would be called *In Great Company*, I found the title immensely fitting. I've known Louis for over 20 years. I respect his work and admire his approach because it is based on his extensive experience working with CEOs and HR leaders to help them create a workplace where people love to be and do their best. As CEO of the Best Practice Institute and one of my Top 100 Coaches, Louis understands that being "in great company" is not about workplace perks or even pay. It is about leaders doing the right thing, showing respect, and empowering people to succeed on a daily basis. These seemingly simple ideas are very difficult to implement.

Luckily, *In Great Company* offers a practical plan to help leaders at all levels make the commitment to ongoing improvement and organizational change. I believe that it will become a valuable addition to leadership and management literature because it combines strategic and human elements of management, and it adheres to some of the ideals that I value most:

> ▶ **Lead with respect.** The central finding in Louis's research, the main idea upon which this book is based, is that people require one thing in order to be at their best at work: *respect*. All of my work coaching top CEOs tells me that this is correct—leaders need to act with humility, become effective listeners, and value the expertise of the people around them. These things signal respect, and they bring out the best in everyone.
>
> ▶ **Set people up to succeed.** Whether your objective is to design team goals or to sell people on a new strategy, *In Great Company* puts the alignment of shared values at the center

of the endeavor and positions achievement of outcomes as the most important task at hand. The type of alignment Louis describes not only makes success easier to measure but also brings more people in the organization into the process and helps them focus on the future.

▶ **Listen and learn.** I teach my clients to ask key stakeholders for suggestions on how they can become more effective leaders. I tell them to listen to these ideas and think about them in order to keep doing what works and let go of what does not. Similarly, one of the central elements of being In Great Company is creating an environment in which we look to the people around us for coaching and feedback to build on our strengths, fix what is broken, and focus on becoming better than ever in the future.

▶ **Change yourself first.** This book is designed to create an emotional connection among employees—one that fosters a shared passion for excellence. Yet, as you will see, it starts with leaders and filters down and across the organization. This ethos of personal discovery and ongoing improvement resonates with me. I believe that one of the most impactful aspirations any of us can have is to become a better version of ourselves. When we are open to change and improvement, it encourages others in the organization to do the same.

Louis has studied organizations. He understands what they do well and what they don't do well. He is an expert on multiple facets of developing people. With considerable research and practice behind him, I can say this is his best work yet. This is an approach that, with practice, can elevate performance, improve retention, and have a positive impact on business outcomes. And by practicing the prescriptions in this book, people can be their best at work, become emotionally connected to each other, and truly feel like they are In Great Company.

—Marshall Goldsmith, *August 2018*

ACKNOWLEDGMENTS

Thank you to Jacqueline Murphy, Marshall Goldsmith, Michael Varouhas, Noah Schwartzberg, and Scott Baxt who were instrumental in making *In Great Company* happen.

THE IN GREAT COMPANY ADVANTAGE

What if we could create a world of work where employees were so deeply engaged that they loved doing their job every day? What if they were so invested in building a better workplace for themselves and others that putting in the extra effort was virtually guaranteed? And what if they could focus so exclusively on doing what's right for customers that profits were essentially a by-product of the process? This would be a place where people were dedicated to working toward collective success. Where mutual respect was the norm and all people felt heard. Everyone would be excited, eager, and poised to collaborate to achieve objectives that they all believed in (Figure I.1).

I can envision this world because I have spent the last 15 years creating a path to make it happen. I call it being "In Great Company." You are In Great Company when you experience a spark that lights your desire for peak performance. This spark comes from the deep emotional connection you feel to your company and the people with whom you work.

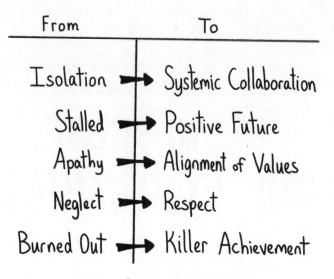

From	To
Isolation	Systemic Collaboration
Stalled	Positive Future
Apathy	Alignment of Values
Neglect	Respect
Burned Out	Killer Achievement

FIGURE 1.1 *Being In Great Company*

As founder and CEO of the Best Practice Institute (BPI) and as an executive coach and organizational psychologist, I spend my day working with leaders to help them ignite their spark. The psychologist in me dives down to diagnose problems and identify opportunities, while the executive coach in me formulates a practical action plan to help leaders discover how they can become better through feedback and the power of their stakeholder, peer, or customer network.

The In Great Company approach I describe throughout this book is based largely on my work with the Best Practice Institute, a leadership development and solutions center for senior talent and human resources (HR) executives. As a subset of that, I formed the BPI Talent Consortiums, otherwise known as the Senior Executive Board (SEB). The SEB is a leadership experience where C-level leaders can come together to be In Great Company—surrounded by supportive peers who care about each other's growth and share similar goals. These experiences include curated conversations, custom research on current challenges, provocative online learning, and in-person venues where leaders meet with industry colleagues and stakeholders to share best and next practices, hold each other accountable for objectives, publish important new findings, and collaborate to solve larger national and world issues.

The BPI Senior Executive Board formed in New York City in 2001 after the 9/11 attacks as a way to reconnect to our passions and become even more successful *together*. Since then, we often assemble executives from the same value chain to solve stubborn challenges and support each other's growth. Other times, it is industry "competitors" coming together to share insights and advice. We have met at the United Nations to discover how to become more sustainable and socially responsible. And we've met at the Pentagon to dive into veteran hiring processes with top-level officials.

To further this work, we came back to Manhattan on the tenth anniversary of the 9/11 attacks, where I led an especially memorable executive session. The venue overlooked the site of Ground Zero from the executive dining room of Manhattan's Westin New York at Times Square. Many of the leaders at the BPI Senior Executive Board meeting had lost family members, close friends, and colleagues. They opened up about deeply personal moments in their lives and shared stories until the early hours of the morning. We talked about how our personal feelings and experiences affect our mindset and motivation at work. As you can imagine, there were tears flowing, and peers provided support. We closed the restaurant with the staff that evening, leaving as a strong group, intact and in solidarity. We were no longer just colleagues, we felt bound together like a family.

Not every interaction at work can or should be like that one, but when employees connect to each other in a deeper way, and when they feel supported by leaders and able to be themselves, it alters their perception of their workplace. It creates the positive dynamic that I call "being In Great Company." When you are In Great Company, you are in a place you love to be, you choose to add value, and you want to give more of yourself. As a result, you are more willing and able to achieve your business goals.

You can be In Great Company by sparking deeper emotional connections with colleagues—by aligning your values, collaborating, cocreating a positive future, giving respect, and focusing on achievement. When this dynamic is set into motion in the workplace, everyone is aligned and willing to do whatever it takes to preserve and grow the business together. It is a scenario in which everyone wins.

The Core of In Great Company: Emotional Connectedness

Every program I have implemented and all of the advice and cases in my 10 previous books have been aimed at creating a workplace people love and funneling their positive feelings to set up the entire business for sustainable success. Yet, I am also a data junkie. I feel compelled to examine the facts before I can move from theory to action. I use data to identify best practices and write cases that generalize what I have learned. That is how I made a discovery— one that changed my thinking about what people really want from work and what motivates them to be their best.

It started with one simple question about being In Great Company. As part of my research initiative, I asked 100 executives: *"What is the one factor you need most from an employer to motivate your performance and help you be great at your job?"*

As a recovering skeptic (it's a daily battle), I fully expected the majority of people to suggest that the key factor for motivating great performance would be a massive salary increase, followed by flextime and fancy perks like foosball tables or swing sets in the cafeteria. Instead, an overwhelming number of people aligned around a factor that was far from what I expected: 9 out of 10 people said the one thing that would motivate high performance was a "feeling of respect." They were looking for respect in the workplace. Well, what do you know?

> "I'm not concerned with your liking or disliking me. . . .
> All I ask is that you respect me as a human being."
> —Jackie Robinson

This surprising finding set me on a learning journey. I went back to the 100 executives to ask them what respect really meant to them. I then talked to over 300 CEOs and chief human resources officers. I conducted countless pulse surveys. I spoke to colleagues and management experts, and I interviewed hundreds of other employees and executives at conferences and as part of my consulting work. I set up executive round tables and worked through these questions with participants.

What I learned through all of this inquiry and synthesis is that respect in the workplace is directly related to a feeling of emotional connectedness. People felt respected when there was an environment of mutual support, a bond of acceptance, values alignment, two-way dialogue, and reciprocal trust. I found that respect enables emotional connection, and emotional connection cultivates respect. This overlap between these two ideas came up again and again.

As I have continued to dig into emotional connectedness in particular, I have found that a great many people in the workplace feel out of sync with the values and practices of their organization. The issue goes beyond incentives. Instead, it is a general misunderstanding about what people want from work. And the disconnect cuts across organizational structure and company culture. We are giving people ways to work more independently through new technology, for example, yet they are yearning to be a part of something larger that connects them to others. We are enabling them to accomplish goals faster and move on, yet they want to collaborate and commit to a long-term purpose that they believe in. We are generating more precise systems for focused goal setting and performance management, yet people want to be trusted and empowered to act on their own to solve problems that mean something to them.

Overall, we are creating tools and programs aimed at delivering on the traditional notion of employee engagement, when what we should be focusing on is creating emotional connectedness. This is the core driver of the In Great Company approach. *Emotional connectedness brings people together in the workplace as almost nothing else can. When employees are emotionally connected, they feel respected, and that drives high performance.*

Emotional connectedness emerged in my research as a valuable lever for performance and engagement—and one that was largely unexplored.

I define *emotional connectedness* (EC) as the sense of belonging that people feel when they see that their work affects organizational outcomes positively and their work matters to their managers, colleagues, and the wider world. It is the motivating sense of satisfaction and intellectual alignment that results from feeling appreciated and part of a purpose that people believe in and have in common with colleagues.

The people in my 9/11 session tapped into the power of emotional connection, but the utility of this idea extends much further than one night or one group of executives. Whether they are producing car parts or conducting research that saves lives, people want to feel emotionally connected within the workplace. They want trust, support, and respect to be defining factors in the place where they spend so many of their waking hours. Emotional connectedness, as part of the larger In Great Company model in this book, offers the tools and mindset we need to bring people together in the workplace to feel happier and motivated to accomplish more with greater collaboration and creativity.

The High Cost of Low EC

What I see in my everyday work with organizations is that many well-intentioned employee engagement programs are having an effect that is the opposite of what they intend. They are making it easier to work efficiently and independently, but they fail to engender satisfaction and happiness at work, and this naturally extends to customers.

THE SOUND OF APATHY IN THE WORKPLACE

These are some of the things people tell me about feeling disconnected in the workplace:

- ▶ "My manager sends directions to me but doesn't provide details, so I am left to read his mind. He gets angry when I don't understand him."
- ▶ "I received a high rank on my annual performance review, but I don't know if anything about my work is actually having an impact."
- ▶ "I think our business is doing well, but I don't know what we stand for or what our strategy is. It feels empty."
- ▶ "I have an idea for a new way of providing extra value to customers based on their feedback to me, but I don't know whom to tell."

I will examine why we crave emotional connectedness in greater detail in Chapter 1, but the short explanation is that we humans have an innate desire to establish and maintain close ties to each other. *The positive news for managers is that emotionally connected employees remain in their jobs longer, perform better, and connect more deeply with customers.* And organizations can take that to the bank: the financial damage incurred to replace employees who leave or are "separated" is high and rising.

For example, studies by the Society for Human Resource Management (SHRM) show that every time a business needs to replace an employee, it costs an average of six to nine months' salary[1] (For a manager making $80,000 a year, that's $40,000 to $60,000.) Other studies indicate that the price tag on ongoing employee turnover is even steeper at the executive level, showing that recruiting, training, and lost productivity can run as high as twice their annual salary.[2]

Perhaps most importantly, I would argue that holding on to employees who are emotionally adrift is perhaps pricier than replacing them when they decide to leave. For instance, people who feel isolated or marginalized are perpetual underperformers. In time, their inertia becomes contagious, and they drag others down with them. In some cases, disconnected leaders create a dysfunctional dynamic that sows discord across their team in a way that eventually extends to stakeholders and customers. In other cases, employees who are undermotivated are less likely to maintain the momentum required to complete projects and close sales. Meanwhile, their colleagues need to work harder to compensate, thereby elevating workplace stress and tension across the board.

In other words, creating emotional connectedness is cost-effective. It is far more productive than traditional engagement programs:

▶ **Attempts at employee engagement underperform.** While 87 percent of organizations list engagement as one of their top priorities,[3] only 15 percent of employees actually report feeling engaged in the workplace.[4] In contrast, emotional connectedness is a lesser-known part of the employee experience that has a higher return on investment. For example, my study showed that employees who were emotionally connected as part of the larger In Great Company model were more likely to perform at higher levels than those who were not, by factor of 4.[5]

▶ **Employee engagement programs offer the wrong incentives.** Most models promote what the organization can "give" to employees to engage them to perform better. For example, an analysis of 51 separate experiments found overwhelming evidence that "incentives may reduce an employee's natural inclination to complete a task and derive pleasure from doing so."[6] My research corroborates this, showing that perk-based plans—even those based on financial incentives—fail to create legitimate buy-in from employees in the long term, despite the cost to employers. The In Great Company model focuses on the intersection between employee practices and organizational structure, whereby employees are given opportunities to work in ways that create a lasting emotional connection to the company. These practices provide a new context for teams and a new contract for organizations to cocreate a positive culture that brings people together.

▶ **Leaders get lost in the typical engagement effort.** Employee engagement programs are largely the responsibility of overworked HR departments. They focus on rolling out annual engagement surveys and providing employees with benefits and options. But very few are set up to ensure that leaders are able and equipped to deliver on what employees really want. Emotional connectedness starts at the top. In fact, leadership development, organizational culture, and management structure are the most important elements of being In Great Company.

I have titled this book *In Great Company* because people who feel genuine emotional connectedness have a deep and abiding love for their workplace. They know they are "In Great Company," and they are therefore willing to contribute the discretionary effort required to take their work to the next level. For instance, my study shows that receiving respect, living the values espoused by the company, and creating a positive, functional, and collaborative community promote love of one's workplace, which translates to increased performance and loyalty. All of these elements are a part of the In Great Company paradigm that we will explore throughout this book.

How to Be In Great Company: Five Elements That Spark Peak Performance

We need to feel connected and respected. This simple statement is at the heart of the employee engagement conundrum. It epitomizes the disconnect that holds companies back from growth and causes individuals to languish and underperform.

It doesn't need to be this way.

Based on long-term research, including four studies of over 3,500 employees, and more than 20 years of collected learnings from dialogue groups and peer coaching C-level executives in hundreds of Fortune 1000 organizations, the best way to achieve next-level engagement and increased productivity is not through salary bumps, Ping-Pong tables, free lunches, or even additional paid leave. It's something much deeper and more intrinsic.

Our myth busting research shows that high performance and engagement occur when people are surrounded by like-minded colleagues who are set up to succeed together and empowered to pursue a common mission. We have found that when employees feel emotionally connected to the workplace and each other in this way, then many other things fall readily into place. *When employees are emotionally connected, they become the hardworking brand ambassadors that every organization needs to succeed.* With emotional connectedness, employees are happier and more willing to contribute extra effort. The best news of all? Emotionally connected employees love their employer, and (based on our survey) they are 94 percent more likely to want to perform better.[7]

But is this fabled state of emotional connectedness really possible? Not only is it possible, it is instrumental to the success of organizations. According to Bob Maresca, CEO of Bose Corporation, "Emotional connectedness undoubtedly inspires discretionary effort and passion from our employees and our customers."[8] Dozens of other top executives have told me the same thing.

The chapters that follow reveal the art and science of sparking a culture of emotional connectedness. With an approach that my colleagues and I field-tested in small, midsized, and Fortune 500 companies and over 40 peer benchmarking groups, this simple, scalable model is built on five dimensions that create psychological safety and a strong sense of belonging.

The five elements are the core of In Great Company, and they are proven to be critical for elevating workplace outcomes including engagement and productivity (Figure I.2). Explored in depth in Chapters 3 through 7, they are ubiquitous, implementation focused, and far more effective then expensive perks. It is these five elements of EC that come together to spark the effect and feeling that we are In Great Company and performing at our peak in the workplace:

1. **Systemic collaboration:** *Collaboration* is a common business buzzword, but *systemic collaboration* is different. It gets to the core of true and functional collaboration—where collaboration becomes a part of the inner workings of the organization and its decision-making processes. Employees are In Great

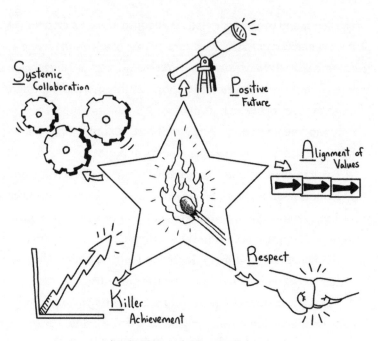

FIGURE 1.2 *The SPARK Model for Peak Performance:*
The Five Elements of EC

Company when they work in small teams and cocreate results
using open communication channels, where information and
advice for being better in the future are shared freely and
frequently. This way of working creates a connection almost
by definition. Taking the idea further to establish an emotional
connection requires the right rule setting and structure. We'll
show with examples from companies including Atlassian and
KeyBank that all teams need several specific practices to
cocreate a sustained connection that drives results.

2. **Positive future:** Employees are In Great Company in progress-
   focused cultures that foster innovation and passion. Because
   positivity is a cultural contagion, emotional connectedness
   is achieved when individuals use it in a unified way to move
   forward together to achieve results. Although positivity may
   seem like a by-product of emotional connectedness, our

study showed that it is also a powerful catalyst for creating an emotionally connected culture. With guiding examples including Big River Steel and WD-40, I will explore the elements of positivity that are emblematic best practices of the In Great Company model.

3. **Alignment of values:** Employees are In Great Company in organizations that place an emphasis on higher-order qualities such as honesty, integrity, and resonance with personal beliefs. The emotional connection is established when leaders and peers all embrace common values and everyone holds each other equally accountable. Granular practices include things as simple as doing what you say you are going to do or speaking truth instead of avoidance and more conceptually complicated practices such as living the values and ethics the company espouses. I will provide the critical tools to put these ideals into practice as well as numerous stories and best practices from Patagonia and Johnson & Johnson.

4. **Respect:** I will show that the sense of emotional connectedness becomes far deeper in environments where respect is established as a type of social currency that is exchanged reciprocally. Making respect a part of the organization's ethos and talent management processes—as Starbucks and Wegmans have—is essential to applying this dimension. I will show why respect is perhaps the most important of the five elements (according to our research, feeling genuinely respected is the number 1 reason people love their workplace and feel that they are In Great Company), and I position it as the element that catalyzes all of the others to drive peak performance. Respect is the match that sparks the flame in the In Great Company model, and it informs the practices that are central to keeping people connected and engaged.

5. **Killer achievement:** Achievements feels hollow unless both the individual and organization experience a benefit. Killer

achievement delivers a combination of financial and emotional upside that amplifies the effect for everyone. Employees are In Great Company in a workplace where people are empowered to focus on the customers and critical goals and when extraneous minutia is eliminated. In this case, emotional connectedness is markedly deepened when people have objectives that are simply stated and the system removes competing interests that block the path to success. The factors critical to this dimension are identifying and measuring the elements that are most important to the organization and allowing easy options for executive coaching, leadership, and organization development. We will look at Netflix and Best Buy, among many other guiding examples of the achievement element, where people create killer outcomes that keep the organization relevant, strong, and innovative.

These five practices, as part of the larger In Great Company context, provide a new framework for teams and organizations to co-create a positive culture that brings people together. As we will see, the success of each of these elements is in the frequency of follow-up and measurement of change that occur as a result of practice and development. With real examples from my work with companies that serve to bring these elements to life, this book places employees in the driver's seat and makes them active participants in their own quest for satisfaction and high performance.

The best practices in this book are the ubiquitous drivers of a culture that create intensely positive feelings within the workplace, engage people to produce more, and ultimately provide greater profit. The chapters ahead offer not only a research-based roadmap for making emotional connectedness manageable but also the tools we need right now to bridge the engagement divide and keep people striving to work together to create a workplace where everyone is In Great Company.

About the Chapters

▶ **Chapter 1:** Before we examine the elements of In Great Company, Chapter 1 digs deeper into emotional connectedness and interacts with key concepts, including psychological safety, affective commitment, and emotional intelligence. Understanding these conceptual underpinnings will make it easier for you to apply this new model and use it to create a results-driven workplace where people love to be.

▶ **Chapter 2:** The next step in execution is for you to examine the In Great Company model all together through the lens of leadership. "The Emotionally Connected Leader" looks at how you can make the most of In Great Company by setting the tone from the top down. Creating emotional connectedness is everyone's job, but leadership buy-in and focus will be your most critical element of success.

▶ **Chapters 3 through 7:** Each chapter explores a single element individually and in depth, including why it works and how to apply it. For each element, a Best Practices Playbook guides you on how to implement each component of the In Great Company model.

▶ **Chapter 8:** With all of the knowledge, examples, and advice at your fingertips and fresh in your mind, Chapter 8, "Conclusion," points you to the "Five Things to Do Right Now" to be In Great Company on day one.

CHAPTER 1

MAXIMIZING THE EC EQUATION

My professional quest to create emotional connectedness coincides with my personal passion for drumming. I have played drums professionally and continue to play in a band. As is true for all lifelong musicians, music is part of what defines me as a person. I crave the creative outlet and appreciate the way that music inspires people to come together to connect around the art. After 9/11, for example, I was in New York earning my master's degree in organizational leadership at Columbia University. At the time, it did not require any special insight to understand why so many of us in the city and across the country felt bereft and alone in our grief and loss. As a way to connect with others and exchange emotional support, I created and facilitated a campus drum circle that suddenly became popular around New York City. It was transformative for me to see how creating an emotional connection with other drummers based on shared values and interests can align and motivate people in a very positive way.

I look at drumming as a tool that helps people shed the exterior veneers that get in the way of connecting with each other on an emotional level. Instead of constantly striving or comparing accomplishments (how much money you make, what kind of car you drive, if you own a vacation home, and so on), we are all the same in the context of a drum circle. We all become drummers. Today I also volunteer as a drummer for nonprofit and educational events as a way to connect kids to learning opportunities and inspire them to come together to celebrate their uniqueness. For me, drumming connects me to the audience and my fellow musicians in a way that little else does. And I am always searching for ways to funnel that advantage into organizations as a coach and organizational psychologist. It is no surprise to me, then, that emotional connectedness is the secret sauce that makes In Great Company sustainable as a management model.

EC is effective and enduring because it provides people with innate benefits that they need to feel complete, connected, and uber-motivated to perform at their very best. I will mention these benefits in this chapter, in part to show how they yield equally pertinent payback for individuals and organizations.

As a part of a mutually reinforcing dynamic, it's important to understand that emotional connectedness is both reciprocal and cumulative. It is reciprocal because organizations receive employee loyalty, intense initiative, and goal alignment in exchange for the effort they invest in the approach. Likewise, it is cumulative because the more EC you create among employees, the better the benefits. For example, the full model has five prescriptive elements (examined in Chapters 3 through 7). Each creates and deepens connections between employees and their workplace and motivates people to succeed. Yet, to achieve the In Great Company ideal, organizations need to pursue the prescriptions that pertain to all five elements of the model.

Benefits of Emotional Connectedness

With emotional connectedness as the benefit, the payback is well worth the investment in time and effort. Figure 1.1 lists the specific benefits you can expect.

FIGURE I.I

EC Fulfills Intrinsic Needs

As mentioned, EC surpasses the typical goals for employee engagement that organizations aspire to achieve. In fact, Abraham Maslow's famous Hierarchy of Needs, the theory of psychological health that ranks the innate drivers of self-actualization, mentions a sense of belonging as a basic element that motivates human behavior, just above food, shelter, and safety.[1] Numerous recent studies, as well, show that EC is a prerequisite that people need to thrive. It improves physical health, for example, with one study showing that social and emotional connectedness increases longevity.[2] Conversely, numerous studies report that the lack of social and emotional support can elevate the risk of heart disease, diabetes, and obesity.[3]

Emotional connectedness has a similarly positive impact on psychological well-being and mental health. For instance, Emma Seppälä of the Stanford Center for Compassion and Altruism Research and Education, and the author of *The Happiness Track*, wrote, "People who feel more connected to others have lower levels of anxiety and depression. Moreover, studies show they also have higher self-esteem, greater empathy for others, are more trusting and cooperative and, as a consequence, others are more open to trusting and cooperating with them."[4]

Dr. Seppälä went on to explain: "Social connectedness generates a positive feedback loop of social, emotional, and physical well-being."[5]

While all of this rigorous research is validating, it is arguably easy to believe, based on personal experience, that emotional support and healthy social connections have vital business benefits. Most of us crave emotional connectedness—in part because our lives depend on it. And the rewards for connecting employee health and well-being to emotional connectedness are significant. According to a survey of 361 companies and 3,822 employees, nearly 87.4 percent of respondents said that wellness positively affected work culture, and 88 percent described access to health and wellness programs as an important factor for defining an employer of choice.[6]

The few organizations today that do manage to factor the intrinsic needs of employees into their value proposition—Barry-Wehmiller and Wegmans are two that we will look at in detail in the chapters that follow—have benefited in numerous ways from employee retention and increased productivity to positive PR with customers and a strong corporate culture. If nothing else, it is important to know that the In Great Company approach offers a way to build basic human experience into business, and it does so in part because without that, success and progress are impossible to achieve.

EC Makes Emotional Intelligence More Actionable

Emotional intelligence is arguably one of the most important and transformative leadership ideas in recent history. First introduced into the academic literature in the late 1980s and early 1990s, psychology professors Peter Salovey and John Mayer introduced the concept as a type of social intelligence, separate from general intelligence. According to them, emotional intelligence (EI) "includes the ability to engage in sophisticated information processing about one's own and others' emotions and the ability to use this information as a guide to thinking and behavior. That is, individuals high in emotional intelligence pay attention to, use, understand, and manage emotions."[7]

In 1990, the American psychologist Daniel Goleman popularized emotional intelligence as part of leadership practice in an article for *Harvard Business Review* and later in several popular books. In his work, Goleman outlined five domains of EI: self-awareness, self-regulation, internal motivation, empathy, and social skills.[8] Work on emotional intelligence by Goleman and others was both relevant to leadership practice and also groundbreaking in the leadership lexicon because it was among the first ideas to integrate and synthesize psychology and cognitive science as part of management theory. The famous and highly respected Jack Welch, who was passionate about developing leaders at GE during his heyday as CEO, has said, "Emotional intelligence is more rare than book smarts, but my experience says it is actually more important in the making of a leader. You just can't ignore it."[9]

Yet, emotional intelligence has also been criticized for being a "softer side" management idea (right brain theory) and therefore less relevant in strategy, operations, and analytical or logic-based management areas that are commonly associated with driving business results.

Inasmuch as EI theory is still evolving, *I would argue that emotional connectedness takes the landmark idea of emotional intelligence further by using new research to identify tangible takeaways and building additional actionable practices around it.* Like EI, emotional connectedness is measurable. But unlike EI, emotional connectedness is in no way fixed as part of one's natural personality, ability, or intelligence. Emotional intelligence can be honed and practiced, to be sure, but it is arguably as much about nature as nurture. In contrast, emotional connectedness is achieved by putting five specific elements into practice. EC is more specific than emotional intelligence, and it also serves to broaden EI's applications and frameworks for ongoing practice and measurement. In short, the prescriptions in this book provide additional tools for making EI more actionable and beneficial to enlightened organizations.

Some companies consciously include EI as part of their hiring criteria, and many more attempt to measure emotional intelligence in their performance management systems. The benefits are clear—research shows that 90 percent of top performers are skilled at managing their emotions.[10] Using a focused, practical approach, the In Great Company model offers a proactive way to weave emotional connectedness across all aspects of the organization and make it a cultural imperative.

EC Creates Psychological Safety

A few years back, I was brought in to observe a privately owned industrial manufacturing firm that had recently hired new managers to accelerate growth. Having survived the Great Recession in better shape than its competitors, the owners saw a window of opportunity to build the business. The new managers were experienced in the industry and comfortable implementing a growth strategy. They pressed ahead aggressively. Less than a year later, the business was going in the wrong direction—sales had slowed and longtime employees were leaving in waves. When I came in to help diagnose the problem, interviews with employees revealed that the issue had nothing to do with the aggressive strategy shift. Instead, the new leaders had created an environment that one employee aptly called "inhospitable." They were systematically excluding existing employees from key decisions and creating a climate of fear for "old guard" team leaders. The loss of psychological safety had brought collaboration to a halt, and the whole business was suffering as a result.

It became apparent to me, from this experience and others like it, that organizational imperatives like collaboration and experimentation can be effective only when individuals feel secure enough to cocreate, share ideas, and offer advice without fear of reprisal. This elemental observation correlates with a noted two-year study conducted by Google in 2015 that looked at 250 attributes of teams and found that psychological safety was one of several dynamics that set successful teams apart from other teams at Google. The company found that the safer team members felt with one another, the more likely they were to admit mistakes, partner, and take on new roles.[11] Paul Santagata, head of industry at Google, summed it up like this: "There's no team without trust."[12]

Indeed, psychological safety delivers a positive physiological response in humans, neutralizing the fight-or-flight response that may otherwise occur when we feel vulnerable during interpersonal interactions, freeing us up to contribute fully and openly. Harvard professor Amy Edmondson, who coined the term "psychological safety" in a study published in 1999 and who has pioneered the modern theory and practice associated with this idea, has said that psychological safety brings "a sense of confidence that the team will not embarrass, reject or punish someone for speaking up."[13] With this, psychological safety yields not only trust but also inclusion and diversity, as more of us are willing to be fully present in groups and express diverse perspectives that others can learn from.

In my work as a coach and organizational psychologist, *I have seen what creating an atmosphere of psychological safety can do: markedly improve engagement, allow people to learn and grow, drive creativity and innovation, and even turn failing organizations around.* It is that powerful and important.

As an essential part of the In Great Company approach, emotional connectedness serves to embed psychological safety into the fabric of an organization's practices in active ways while also creating a challenging environment that motivates people to perform. This key dynamic of EC affects people and performance in a positive way, and it is one of the most singularly robust levers for innovation that I have experienced in my career.

EC Drives Discretionary Effort

The fourth positive dynamic created by emotional connectedness is affective commitment. This is where the rubber meets the road, and EC creates meaningful engagement, improves retention, and drives voluntary discretionary effort. In other words, it creates value and drives results.

Defined as an employee's positive emotional attachment to the organization,[14] *affective commitment* creates a sense of belonging that increases our desire to have an impact, enhances our willingness to pursue shared goals, and elevates our desire to remain with the organization.[15] *Driven in part by reciprocity, affective commitment is created and elevated when employees believe that the company is committed to their success and well-being.* In essence, affective commitment is itself an emotional bond.

The most notable part of affective commitment is what it nurtures. First, it creates an ownership dynamic where employees feel responsible for the success of the business. According to research, having a sense of psychological ownership makes employees more willing to work harder and work on behalf of the organization and its employees. It improves job satisfaction, initiative, and ultimately work performance as well.[16] Affective commitment also leads employees to contribute greater "voluntary discretionary effort" and to be willing to go above and beyond what is required or expected. Studies show that the "we are in this together" element of affective commitment makes people "work better, longer and enjoy it more."[17]

As an emotional attachment, affective commitment is a result of EC, but it also helps to create it. Because the In Great Company dynamic is about mutual commitment by employees and the organization, it is the reciprocity factor that makes it so powerful and sustainable.

Barriers to Creating a Connection

With four core benefits hanging in the balance, there must also be corresponding challenges to achieving EC, or (let's face it) every organization would already be In Great Company.

I will mention how to overcome common challenges in each of the prescriptive chapters that follow. More generally, the big three speed bumps are the same ones that come up again and again in organizational change and transformation efforts: leadership, culture, and structure.

Leadership

Emotional connectedness is an all-in endeavor. The five elements of EC create a type of roadmap for implementation, and every employee needs to be a believer. Yet, it is leaders who are the make-or-break protagonists. Top-down support, sponsorship, and participation can either accelerate or obliterate attempts to make this cultural shift succeed in a sustainable way.

Resistance or simple apathy can come from any level of leadership. Line managers may have competing priorities. Middle managers may set a poor example. C-suite executives might withhold their support, thereby stopping EC in its tracks. The simple solution? Emotional connectedness needs to be a leadership priority.

Culture

As the aphorism goes, culture eats strategy for breakfast.[18] In other words, EC as part of the In Great Company approach looks amazing on paper, but proper implementation calls for cultural readiness. As mentioned, supportive leadership is a part of this readiness. In addition, the norms and attitudes that define an organization must be open to emotional connectedness or able to change.

Cultural compatibility is a sticky wicket because EC always requires some degree of change—and not all organizations are prepared for it. The most common reason companies engage in the difficult work of culture change is because a turnaround is called for—but a better path is to remain ahead of the curve and start before the transformation is necessary.

Structure

The five elements of EC— systemic collaboration, positive future, alignment of values, respect, and killer achievement—are easier to implement when an organization's structure is open and flexible. While a big part of the In Great Company approach is aimed at incremental changes that deliver adaptability and transparency, the reality is that bureaucratic structures make it more difficult to implement this or any new management approach. Conversely, efficient, flexible organizational structures that are open to empowering people dramatically accelerate implementation efforts.

A New Competitive Advantage

Managing the emotional culture within your organization may seem novel if not outright unexpected. That is exactly why this practice offers a competitive advantage—because it is innovative and disruptive. With typically grim statistics on "engagement" coming from Gallup and SHRM,[19] creating emotional connectedness is an opportunity to think differently and have a positive impact on employee commitment, happiness, and performance.

You will likely see yourself and your colleagues reflected in the dozens of anecdotes and examples contained in this book. These are large organizations and small companies; they are global multinationals and local nonprofits. The common denominator between them all? The human factor. Thanks to advancements in technology and digital infrastructure, we can all connect to each other easily all the time. Yet, that connection is superficial and largely pragmatic. Emotional connectedness puts people In Great Company because it taps into a deeper, more meaningful way of working together and motivating people to perform. It is more effective because it allows people to put their inner selves into their work. In doing so, it leverages the human experiences—something powerful that frequently gets hidden away within organizations. Focusing on EC is a dramatically different way to approach the workplace, and you can expect dramatically better results—results that objectively elevate engagement and make companies more competitive, customer centric, and successful.

That is the ultimate takeaway of this book—to help organizations and the people within them to become more successful. We will begin with the people who help set the stage and set the standard for being In Great Company: leaders.

CHAPTER 2

THE EMOTIONALLY CONNECTED LEADER

People who are In Great Company love their workplace. And it shows in everything they do. They make decisions that add value, strive to perform better, and work in collaboration with colleagues to cocreate a company that achieves great results for customers. More than anything, the emotional connection they feel in the workplace is the driving force that motivates them to perform at their peak every day.

The reinforcing dynamic of EC, whereby the more that people contribute, the greater their payback, is as vibrant and relevant at the leadership level as it is across the rest of the company. In fact, I would argue that leaders are the most important piece of the In Great Company puzzle for a few clear and compelling reasons.

First, leaders need to be the champions of change for any effort to take hold and take off. As change expert John Kotter has established in his work, it is the leaders' responsibility to formulate a vision, communicate the change to the organization, and ultimately create a sense of urgency that generates the momentum a transformation needs to succeed.[1] Next, leaders must be role models who set the behavioral norms for others to follow. When leaders introduce and authentically adapt a transformation like this one, their buy-in helps to enroll others, create a culture shift, and build a coalition of support. Organizational change is viewed as risky, so leaders need to be out in front to create the psychological safety that encourages others to proceed. Last, organizational transformations are delicate to begin with. The commonly accepted data point is that 70 percent of all change efforts fail. If that's true, then the 30 percent that succeed in a sustainable way are doubtless those that are being driven by dedicated leaders.

More specifically, the In Great Company promise—that emotional connectedness among employees can create a workplace where people are so deeply engaged and aligned that they are willing do whatever it takes to grow the business together—is not possible without leaders. In fact, when leaders are disengaged, their apathy infects the organization like a virus. People "quit their bosses, not their jobs" for good reason. Everything leaders do is magnified. Every word and action by leaders, good or bad, has an outsized impact on the rest of the organization. With that, emotionally connected leaders make it possible for the In Great Company effort to succeed.

A leader who proceeds In Great Company is more productive, more effective with delegation, sells more, markets better, and is a magnet for other employees who want to learn, grow, and perform at a higher level. In my work with CEOs and CHROs, the majority confirm that they achieve their goals faster (and with less resistance) when they lead with a love for their company and with a feeling of emotional connectedness to their team and employees.

But being In Great Company is not for passive leaders who wait for opportunities. It's for those who are committed to working hard doing what is right and then reaping the benefits. In Great Company leaders lead with emotional connectedness first— they respect and are respected by followers, and in return followers perform better for them. Being In Great Company requires the ability to collaborate effectively, have a future focus, align with your company's values, create an environment of respect with others, and commit to achieving killer outcomes. You need to be hungry, active, and ready.

In Figure 2.1 I've sketched out what the emotionally connected leader looks like. The remainder of this chapter shows how to achieve the ideal, relevant to each of the five elements of In Great Company. As part of that, I have also included the prescriptive models I use with leaders to help focus their efforts. This includes guiding questions that link to core concepts given in Chapters 3 through 7 and the prescriptive playbook that sparks the In Great Company transformation across organizations.

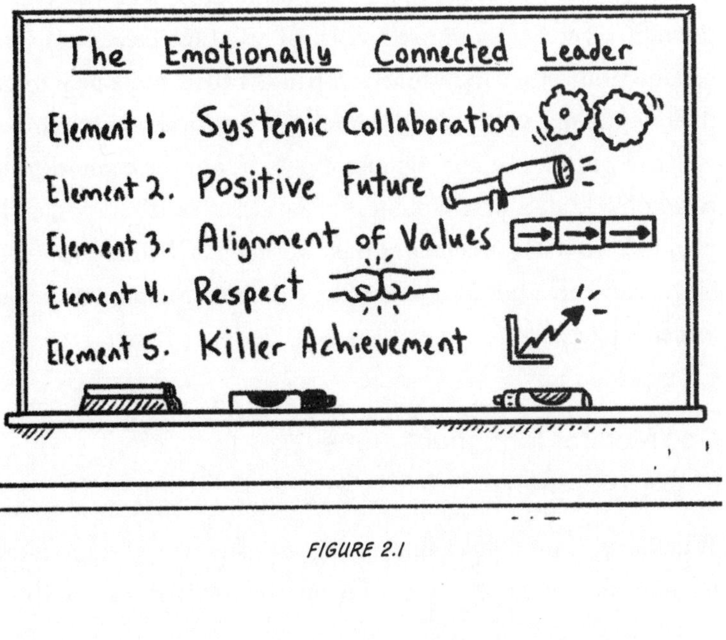

FIGURE 2.1

Element 1. Systemic Collaboration

Do I Insist on Fairness and Full Participation?

Collaboration is not always part of the natural order in leadership. Corporate structure, bureaucracy, politics, and simple inertia can work against it. Yet, we know from the research mentioned in Chapter 3 that organizations that set people up to collaborate are better able to succeed. For that reason, *leaders need to not only inspire collaboration but also insist upon it from others. They need to get beyond the rhetoric to make collaboration a priority*—and many of the best leaders do.

Apple CEO Tim Cook, for instance, has said that leaders can enable collaboration by "looking for people who privately celebrate an achievement but do not care that their name is the one in the lights, . . . people who appreciate different points of view."[2] Former IBM CEO Sam Palmisano said, "The key is to listen. . . . You can't have a dominant point of view because you won't get to the right answers."[3] And Jive Software CEO Elisa Steele said, "For collaboration, the environment for individuals to be able to get their work done with ease and simplicity is critically important."[4]

There is not just one right way to do it, but these emotionally connected leaders have a point of view about collaboration and a plan to keep it at the center of their businesses. What's your plan? Start with these questions to make collaboration a part of your leadership legacy.

Do I Monitor for Equal Airtime in Conversations?

Whether you are a CEO, line manager, or any type of team leader, the most fundamental way to set people up to collaborate is to give them a chance to speak up and express their ideas without fear of recrimination. This means having zero tolerance for conversation hogs, bullies, and time wasters in meetings. It also means making it clear that everyone is expected to participate—no excuses.

How Present Am I During Conversations?

I frequently see leaders who ask a question and then interrupt before their colleague is finished responding. Does this sound like you? Regardless of why it happens (time constraints, lack of emotional intelligence), this bad behavior closes off collaboration. If you are authentic in your desire to be a collaborative leader, you need to keep an open mind, actively listen, and exhibit open, impassive body language that signals you are serious about hearing multiple perspectives before making a decision.

Do I Make Functioning Teams a Priority?

Collaborative leaders know that empowered teams can solve problems, generate new ideas, and manage projects efficiently. As a leader, your job is to design the rules so that teams can function collaboratively. For instance, have you eliminated needless silos? Empowered teams to act within guidelines? Set up an open dialogue and systems for sharing information and expertise? Provided the right tools and technology for collaboration? Perhaps most importantly, have you gotten out of the way to let your teams do their job?

Do I Make Difficult Interactions a Positive Experience?

Collaboration can get messy. Multiple perspectives and differing points of view sometimes surface emotional reactions and dysfunctional dynamics. Therefore, one of the most critical competencies

STAIRWAY TO COLLABORATION

Whether an interaction is complex or routine, running through this Stairway to Collaboration model (Figure 2.2) offers a simple framework for successful collaboration.[5] Each of the six stairs may seem familiar to you because they connect back to other EC elements.

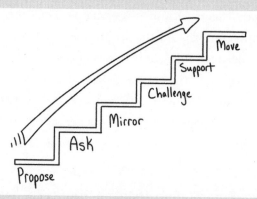

FIGURE 2.2

Source: The Stairway to Collaboration figure and practice are inspired by a coaching model that Deborah Slobodnik taught me that is based on the Four-Player Model—the core concept of David Kantor's theory of structural dynamics published here: David Kantor, *Reading the Room: Group Dynamics for Coaches and Leaders*, Jossey-Bass/Wiley, San Francisco, 2012.

1. First, propose your idea to the team, including scope and what you want to accomplish.
2. Ask for feedback and advice, keeping an open mind.
3. Mirror back the advice and express gratitude.
4. Challenge yourself to see the other person's viewpoint, even if it seems uncomfortable. Ask yourself in earnest, "What can I take away from this advice?"
5. Decide what next step you want to take, and gain support from others—stakeholders, team members, customers, peers, bosses, and more. Listen to their reactions, make

> adjustments accordingly, and allow others to share ownership of the decision.
> 6. Finally, move on the changes. Enlist the help of others to make them happen. Continue to connect it to stakeholders with updates and follow-up.

leaders can model is the ability to manage difficult conversations without drama. Collaborative leaders resolve conflicts and settle differences in a positive and upbeat way with empathy as opposed to enmity.

Amazon's Jeff Bezos put it like this: "Disagree and commit." By way of explanation, he said, "It's a genuine disagreement of opinion, a candid expression of my view, a chance for the team to weigh my view, and a quick, sincere commitment to go their way."[6] In other words, leaders need to listen carefully, express their opinion, and then make a call about how to act. After that, everyone supports the decision regardless of what "side" of the dispute they were on—no drama and no hard feelings.

Element 2. Positive Future

Am I Passionate, Forward Facing, and Eager to Innovate?

Emotionally connected leaders have a positive future outlook when they are passionate about their work, innovative, and focused on the future.

It is no surprise that so many of the CEOs who are highly rated on Glassdoor's "Employees' Choice" survey year after year are innovative, passionate, and future-focused leaders with a unique and positive vision for their company's future.[7] Salesforce founder and CEO Marc Benioff, for example, has been able to articulate a uniquely visionary and future-focused strategy in an incredibly fast-moving and complex industry. Benioff, arguably more than almost any other CEO in the post–Great Recession decade, has famously demonstrated the ability to drive dramatic business shifts and lead employees into the future through constant change and innovation.[8] Even better, he manages business advancement while also giving back to society through the Salesforce Foundation, which has become a role model for other organizations interested in delivering social change. Unsurprisingly, 97 percent of Salesforce employees in Glassdoor surveys approve of Benioff's leadership.

In Chapter 4, we will look at why a positive future vision is one of the main elements of emotional connectedness. The bottom line is that an upbeat outlook is "positively" contagious, and it motivates people to change for the better to be their best. This future focus by leaders is crucial because passion and positivity inspire people almost more than anything else.

Do I Leverage My Personal Passion and Encourage Employees to Do the Same?

When we think of charismatic leaders in business and society, we often attribute some of their success to passion. Martin Luther King Jr. was passionate about equality and civil rights. Henry Ford was passionate about advancing automobile manufacturing. Bill Gates was passionate about personal computers. And so on. In these cases, and others, the connection between passion and a positive future is straightforward. First, passion will sustain you and propel you past innumerable setbacks. Second, it will inform your vision and help you sell your ideas to other people. Finally, passion will connect you to like-minded employees and stakeholders who will help you achieve audacious goals.

Fueled by a passion, you are far more likely to tap into the resilience you need to lead. In addition, if you can engender passion in others, you will surround yourself with the support you need to move toward a positive future.

Do I Have a Positive Relationship with Change?

Leaders who have a knack for change are in a better position to make the numerous shifts needed to keep an organization moving in a progressive trajectory. Benioff makes change look easy at Salesforce. Likewise, Jeff Bezos shifted Amazon from online books to full scale e-commerce to bricks and mortar and back again—almost effortlessly. These leaders are all about change: they know that staying the same is far riskier than experimenting with change.

Even if your relationship with change is not quite as effortless, you need to have your game face ready for change. As mentioned above, change is a top-down endeavor. You need to be the one to envision the change, clearly communicate what it looks like, and be the organization's first and best change champion. Only then can you expect everyone around you—employees, partners, and customers—to take their turn and "stick the landing" of transformation.

Do I Enable and Champion Innovation?

Progress is a main lever for individual happiness. It engages and motivates people and keeps organizations moving forward. Giving people a path and process for innovation, then, will provide you with yet another lever for sparking an emotional connection-through positive future. Enabling innovation has numerous paths: empowering people to propose new ideas, incentivizing them to solve seemingly intractable customer problems, and even investing in notable new ventures on the side.

POSITIVE FUTURE DESIGN GRID

To create a positive future vision for yourself, you need to let go of things from your past that are holding you back and leverage those that serve you well. The Positive Future Design Grid in Figure 2.3 will help you along in this process.

FIGURE 2.3

First, honestly assess how you view yourself. What negative feelings and behaviors from the past can you let go? What positive traits, beliefs, and experiences can you build on? Next, engage in the same clear-eyed assessment to determine how others perceive you. Ask for feedback. What can you shed, and what should you leverage? Finally, consider where you are now and where you want to be. Use that grid to envision a positive future and put a plan together to get there.

The leaders who do it best tend to enable innovation on all levels. No matter what it looks like, your job as a leader is to create the guidelines and guardrails that help people experiment and manage the risk appropriately. Institutionalizing innovation not only removes the fear of failure. It also starts to instill the positive future ethos into your organization's cultural DNA.

Am I a Positive Force for Emotional Connection?

While the concept of creating a positive future is not about being a positive and upbeat person per se, the reality is that leaders who spark emotional connection tend to be enthusiastically supportive of progress. They drive change, leverage passion, and enable innovation. In other words, they are a positive force.

You usually know it when you are a positive force. You are a leader who asks for feedback, and you are highly rated by employees. You give people credit for their ideas and engender loyalty. And you have zero tolerance for meddling managers who squash enthusiasm and innovation. There is commonality here with the characteristics of emotional intelligence. The difference is that emotional connection means that not only are you high in EI yourself but you also expect others in the organization to exhibit the same affinity for driving forward toward a positive future.

Element 3. Alignment of Values

Do I Do What I Say I Will?

Pepsi's longtime CEO Indra Nooyi, who was widely credited with transforming the beverage maker, has a leadership model she calls the "5Cs": *competency*, *courage and confidence*, *communication skills*, *consistency*, and *moral compass*.[9] She talked about this memorable set of leadership promises in board meetings, blogs, keynote speeches, and interviews. Why? Not so she could "claim credit" for her ideas but so she could put a stake in the ground about her beliefs and hold herself accountable for her actions. And the best part of the 5Cs? They dovetail nicely with Pepsi's corporate values and serve to reinforce her commitment to the institution's cultural norms. In other words, Nooyi walked the talk.

Emotionally connected leaders use values to guide their actions, decisions, and communications and to create a "values chain" whereby employees and partners are in sync as they put these values into practice to engage customers.

There are other leaders who walk the talk the way Nooyi does. Honeywell CEO David Cote refused his annual bonus in 2009 to encourage employees to make sacrifices and embrace austerity in order to avoid layoffs during the Great Recession. WD-40's Garry Ridge, a passionate believer in creating an enjoyable workplace where people "step into the best versions of themselves," hosts an annual award ceremony to hand out awards like "The Mother Teresa," "The Rookie of the Year," "The Unsung Hero," and "The Energizer," to recognize employees for their talents.[10] And the infamous and ingenious Richard Branson? He once dressed as a Virgin Airlines flight attendant—red skirt and all.

These leaders and many like them are living by the norms they want to see reflected in their organizations. They are setting the tone for values alignment across the organization, where employees are all working together to create an emotionally connected culture.

As we see in the above examples, leading for values alignment requires a combination of confidence and competence, not to mention a strong dose of charisma. One of the best ways I know to help leaders model and create values alignment across their company is through guided questions to test and strengthen their EC aptitude. Accordingly, we will use the questions below to explore each of the five EC elements and frame it through a leadership lens.

DO YOUR VALUES ALIGN?

What are your core values, and how do they map with the core values of your organization? Use the Values Pyramid shown in Figure 2.4 as a tool for self-discovery, peer dialogue, performance management, and decision-making.

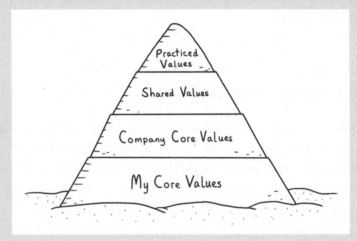

FIGURE 2.4

Once you discover the commonalities that connect your core values with those of your company (and those that are practiced by individuals on your team and elsewhere in your company), you can begin to identify where the agility lies and where you need to achieve greater alignment.

Do I Exemplify Our Corporate Values and Set up Others to Do the Same?

How can you be a leader who walks the talk and inspires others to follow suit? As Nooyi shows with her 5Cs, stepping up to communicate core values (in multiple forms and formats) is the right first step. The next step is demonstrating, through words and actions, that values are mission critical—a priority for you and employees at every level.

In some organizations, the values statement is so concise that leaders can and do recite it frequently. In other cases, leaders mention values explicitly when major decisions are made, making it clear to stakeholders how actions align with the values that define the organization.

Am I Successful in Making a Business Case for the Values of the Company?

Values should guide your decision-making. Without a supporting business case, values are easily set aside when a revenue opportunity presents itself—even one that falls outside the scope of the organization's values comfort zone. Likewise, a business case for values makes the "what's in it for us" clear to employees and customers.

Southwest Airlines, for example, has a clear and convincing business case for its "employees-first" imperative: "We believe that if we treat our employees right, they will treat our customers right, and in turn *that* results in increased business and profits that make everyone happy."[11]

Do I Measure Values Alignment?

Measuring values alignment and using the results as part of your performance management systems rewards employees who are "values champions" and shapes and strengthens the culture. This endeavor should begin during the hiring and onboarding process—using assessments and focused interviews to hire people who are predisposed to share the corporate values—and it should continue as you and other leaders coach employees and provide performance feedback.

Likewise, employees should be able to factor values alignment into 360 feedback for managers. In general, you should put as much effort into measuring and managing values alignment as you put into ensuring business outcomes—because the two are inextricably linked.

Do I Tie Values to Business Strategy?

Values alignment should extend beyond corporate culture to business strategy and decision-making. This act of alignment is the single most important way you can give employees the tools they need to act in ways that reflect shared values.

For example, as we will see in Chapter 5, the Copenhagen-based biotech firm Novozymes embeds its core value—sustainability—into nearly everything it does. It created new businesses around sustainability, for example, and it builds sustainability across its own organization to enable all employees to contribute. In short, sustainability is reflected in Novozymes's purpose, strategy, and long-term targets. The result? There is no doubt the organization has achieved values alignment.

Do I Have Partners to Help Keep Me Accountable for Values?

Through values-focused PR efforts, active discussions, and everyday business practices, you can actively invite customers, vendors, and other stakeholders into the values-alignment effort. Creating this type of business "values chain" strengthens bonds, creates loyalty, and extends emotional connectedness from your workplace to your partners.

Element 4. Respect

Do I Treat Employees Like People?

Bob Chapman, CEO of the private holding company Barry-Wehmiller, has a respect-based management philosophy aimed at making people feel valued and cared for. His human-centric take on leading is designed to "add meaning to people's lives."[12] And Chapman walks the talk. He offers financial incentives to employees who get health screenings, avoids layoffs, and eliminates things (like timeclocks in its factories) that rob people of respect. He avoids demeaning verbiage like "employees" (instead: "team members") and "head count" (instead: "heart count"[13]). Chapman's philosophy has clear commonalities with emotional connectedness—because it makes business better for everyone by basing it on empathy and respect. The result is that 79 percent of team members at Barry-Wehmiller say the company truly cares about them.[14]

Emotionally connected leaders respect differences, consider opinions, treat people with dignity, and understand that they have lives to lead outside of work.

The respect element of emotional connectedness is at the core of everything this book prescribes. It intertwines organizational success and individual empowerment and fulfillment. It also creates a lasting connection between leaders and employees based on what we all have in common—our humanity.

Again, the questions below are designed to test your emotional connectedness and help you develop a leadership style that is based on respect.

Have I Made Respect a Mutual Dynamic?

You may have noticed that people generally agree with you and follow your lead. Guess what? That's not necessarily respect. It's business as usual when you're the boss. Creating mutual respect requires a deeper connection that can be established by engaging in dialogue, asking others for advice, showing your appreciation, and making "regular employees" feel comfortable in your presence. In other words, it requires dedicated effort.

In addition to modeling the behavior you want to see, you also need to hire the right people and design incentives appropriately. Luckily, all of this effort has a big payoff. Respect has a reinforcing effect. When you show respect for employees and design the workplace around it, it sends a signal: everyone is expected to do the same. With persistence, respect becomes a cultural norm (Figure 2.5).

FIGURE 2.5 *The Respect Effect*

Am I Self-Aware? Would Others Say I Am Self-Aware?

A start-up CEO I know told me she was having difficulty with retention. She was stumped. She trained and paid people well, but they were exiting faster than she could recruit replacements. It didn't take long for me to pinpoint the problem. She was a difficult, prickly, and sometimes abusive boss who nonetheless expected people to work long hours under her watchful eye. She showed them scant respect, and she had no idea the disastrous effect it was having on the workplace.

No one *plans* to have a problem with respect. It happens in part because we get so busy steering the ship and creating shareholder value that we lose sight of how we are treating people. This is why self-awareness is so essential for leaders. Cultivating respect to spark emotional connectedness requires knowing how your actions are affecting others and understanding how people perceive you.

The rewards of self-awareness come through a combination of internal and external inputs. *Internal:* Objectively assess your actions, attitudes, and behaviors toward others. You can achieve this by setting time aside, keeping a journal, or otherwise getting in touch with your motivations, triggers, and emotions. *External:* Ask others to tell you the truth about yourself. Solicit anonymous feedback on a regular basis and take it to heart. Over time, if you find that your self-perception is not in sync with how others see you, get coaching, and make the changes you need to create and maintain mutual respect.

Do I Take Inclusion Seriously?

Inclusion is at the very center of respect—respecting people's differences, cultivating their unique strengths, and allowing them to contribute fully and bring their best selves to work. As we will see in Chapter 6, leading for inclusion applies to employees as well as stakeholders such as suppliers and customers.

Leaders who practice, cultivate, measure, and incentivize inclusion at all levels are rewarded with a workforce that is diverse, teams that are empowered and creative, and (according to research) companies that generate great shareholder value.[15] Best of all, they are creating a workplace where people really are In Great Company.

Do I Provide Trust in the Right Balance?

There is no doubt that trust is an essential driver of mutual respect. Yet, like anything else, it can get out of balance. As we have seen, a lack of trust can destroy emotional connectedness. But too much trust? Research shows that an excess of trust, or misplaced trust, can have a negative impact on productivity.[16]

In other words, leaders need to be present, offer positive feedback, and add value. The key is to demonstrate trust through appreciation and empowerment, while also giving people the support and guidance they need to be their best. With this, trust is kept in the right measure as a driver of mutual respect.

Element 5. Killer Achievement

Do I Set People up to Succeed and Achieve?

In *The Seven Habits of Highly Successful People*, arguably the most influential management book of all time, Stephen Covey proposes that we "begin with the end in mind." That simple, brilliant idea offers a path to success that is more memorable than any case study or synthesis of research anywhere.

In my own work with CEOs and CHROs, I have found Covey's idea to be more relevant than ever as we struggle to cope with technological complexity, overlapping objectives, the always-on workforce, and the risk of executive burnout. With this as the backdrop, each of us needs to begin with the end on mind, even as the goalpost constantly pivots and shifts.

Killer achievement is leading with an orientation aimed at accomplishing the maximum results using a focused yet flexible approach to execution that gives employees the support, resources, and motivation they need to achieve.

Emotionally connected leaders cultivate killer achievement, not to create a cutthroat or competitive work environment but to connect people with common goals, set them up to focus on their strengths, and make them more able to master the tasks that matter most. With achievement orientation, when one person succeeds, everyone does. Achievement orientation requires a balance between determination and flexibility because as goals shift, so too must the strategies and training needed to achieve them.

The guiding questions to bring achievement orientation into sharper focus follow.

Do I Create and Communicate Clear, Compelling Goals?

Setting objectives and communicating them crisply is one of the most critical ways you can add value as a leader. Yet, there's much more to the task than that. Emotionally connected leaders think about simplicity, meaning, and empowerment—all things that align people around killer achievement.

Simplicity, first, is critical because goals need to resonate with people in diverse roles and apply to functions across the organization. They need to be easily understood and widely applicable. Next, you need to communicate the big picture or the "why" that is associated with the goal. After all, this critical context is what tells a story and makes goals more meaningful. Finally, you need to enable people to achieve goals in their own way. In other words, goals are tools that should be used as much to empower people as to manage them.

Goals will forever be essential tools in performance management, but emotionally connected leaders view them as another opportunity to bring people together—this time around achievement.

Do I Inspire People to Be Best in Class?

Whether they are farmers or pharmacists, people want their work to matter. In fact, research tells us they need a reason for work that adds meaning to their lives.[17] And what better reason is there than the chance to be a part of something great?

Emotionally connected leaders set people up to achieve great things by motivating them to be "best in class" at what they do. And there are multiple ways to be the best—being first; improving quality, getting great reviews from customers, being innovative, and so on. What this comes down to is that people aspire to high achievement. It is your job as a leader to inspire and equip them to be their best and help them celebrate the small wins that mark steady progress along the way.

Do I Give People the Support
They Need to Achieve?

Setting clear goals and motivating people to go for greatness is a solid start. After that, emotionally connected leaders take the next logical step by giving people the support they need to achieve.

The first level of support is just-right resources. Allocating funding and assigning people in the right measure is as much an art as it is a science—starving projects sets them up to fail, and overfunding creates pressure and stifles experimentation.

Next is development. Study after study shows that employees want training and development options to help them be their best and remain competitive.[18]

Last is moral support. Mentoring, coaching, and carefully facilitated meetings are three ways that emotionally connected leaders enable people to come together to support each other and help one another achieve.

Do I Have a Strengths-Based Approach to Management?

You get the best from everyone when you play to their strengths. Strengths-based leadership cultivates achievement and maximizes resources by leveraging each person's top talents.[19] At times, we have seen organizations that hire people they believe will be a good fit based on culture and skills—even if there's no particular role to fill. The idea is that they will use their strengths proactively to create a role or join a project team that needs their particular strength.

Another moment to focus on strengths is in performance management. As Figure 2.6 shows, achieving a balance in how you structure performance conversations offers a process to focus on appreciating strengths first even as you present the development advice that people need to become better and achieve radical outcomes.

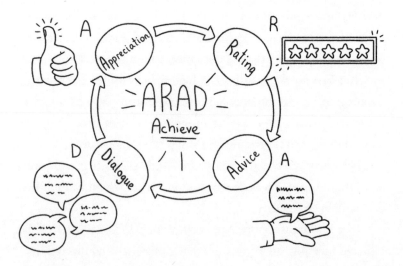

FIGURE 2.6 *The ARAD Model*

Starting with strengths and using appreciation creates lasting connections between leaders and employees and enables people to achieve more based on what they do best. Providing ratings, advice, and a dialogue gives them what they need to accelerate their progress and strengthen their skills and performance.

Do I Balance a Focus on Goals with Flexibility?

Achievement orientation is a path to high performance and a core component of the In Great Company approach. Yet, sustaining achievement and keeping people emotionally connected requires you to build flexibility into the workplace to minimize stress and avoid employee burnout. This imperative brings several ideas together and connects back to the respect element of EC. We need to appreciate employees as people and position flexibility and empathy as levers to keep people connected and able to achieve in a way that leverages their strengths.

Killer achievement is an easy imperative for leaders to champion—but all five elements of EC need to be valued for people to feel respected and connected. The chapters that follow outline each of these elements and prescribe a playbook approach to help leaders spark a cultural high performance that is reinforced by the practices that put people In Great Company.

CHAPTER 3

SYSTEMIC COLLABORATION

Companies that are In Great Company go beyond traditional collaboration. They create systemic collaboration where team-based decision-making, cocreation, and balanced conversation become the hallmark of successful working relationships. *Collaboration* moves from being a buzzword to becoming a part of the fabric of the company's operational infrastructure.

The Dutch banking multinational ING Group took this idea to heart when they eliminated the traditional organization chart over a two-year period beginning in 2016. Since then, everyone works in highly collaborative project teams. Each team has a leader who is responsible for product delivery and a "coach" to make sure the team collaborates effectively. The agile team model employed at ING borrows ideas from Spotify, Netflix, Google, and others. As part of their highly collaborative structure, ING has very few traditional managers, and success depends heavily on trust and transparency within teams. Although their transformation was

admittedly novel—and daring for one of the world's largest financial services and insurance conglomerates—the change was meant
to engage one of their most important stakeholder groups: employees. The result has been improved cycle times, a focus on customer needs, and a company culture that people want to be a part
of.[1] More specifically, the organization credits their collaborative
approach with the following big wins:

1. We are more efficient and more flexible.
2. We can innovate faster with shorter time to market.
3. We are a more attractive employer; our employees
   have much more freedom and responsibility than in a
   traditional company approach.[2]

ING is far from alone in its quest to turbocharge performance
through collaboration. General Electric is also betting its business
on collaboration within and among project teams.[3] As it attempts
to make the difficult shift from being a massive industrial era behemoth to being a lean, digitally enabled enterprise, its leaders have
deemed collaboration to be core to their efforts at reinvention and
transformation. As part of that, much of the GE workforce is now
organized in small, cross-functional groups that huddle with customers and suppliers, utilizing their feedback to optimize their
product development process.[4]

GE and other large organizations are moving to embrace a
more collaborative approach—in this case, *The Lean Startup* approach[5]—that brings people together in new ways. Nick Perugini,
GE's head of commercial digital technology, put it this way: "We
all cross the finish line together, or nobody wins."[6]

Judging by these and other companies that are embarking
on radical change efforts, collaboration has become an aspirational path to renewal and reinvention. In fact, it has become a

catchphrase for everything from Agile software development, crowdsourcing, and cocreation to old-fashioned teamwork. It is also just as much about working together virtually, as is so often the case today, instead of the traditional scrum that starts in a conference room. All of these concepts present useful best practices to pull ideas from, but what we really need from collaboration is something far more focused. With that, I would argue that emotional connectedness may prove to be collaboration's biggest benefit by far.

Why Collaboration Connects Us

Stated simply, *collaboration is when two or more parties work together jointly toward a common objective.* This occurs less often face-to-face and more often cities and countries apart. It also occurs less with traditionally siloed departments and more with multifunctional teams or informal groups bound together by a shared interest. *Instead of delivering pure consensus, collaboration catalyzes innovation and enables people to be more creative and productive.* It is that—working together to be better—that the individuals in my study told me they wanted. I heard loud and clear in my research that people are In Great Company in an open and transparent environment where employees have equal airtime and can abide by simple rules for delivering more value to customers.

These basic deliverables pack a powerful punch. Ample research makes a strong case for collaboration. An ethnographic study conducted by Cisco, for instance, showed that employees value collaboration because the "collective intelligence and diverse perspectives of people working together" creates better overall results.[7] Similarly, a study from Stanford found that working collectively on a task can improve performance. Participants who collaborated persevered 64 percent longer to find solutions than peers who worked individually. They also reported higher engagement and lower fatigue, and they self-reported greater rates of success.[8] On an organizational level, a finding by the Institute for Corporate Productivity, working with social networks expert and Babson College professor Rob Cross, found that high-performance companies are up to 5.5 times more likely to value and reward collaboration.[9]

Whether it's truly a silver bullet for organizational performance or not, collaboration links up nicely with a number of key workforce trends that reflect the way people want to work. Demographics, for one, support streamlined collaboration. Generation Y workers are connected, informed, and solutions focused. They respond universally to coaching and feedback over traditional command-and-control dogma. If they have a problem, they collaborate to solve it, or they extrapolate and find their own fast fix.[10] (Interestingly, even as each new demographic comes colored with a new and different context, so much remains the same—including the challenges of collaboration and every person's need and desire for growth and development.) Next, everyday social networks and collaborative software tools—although themselves always evolving—enable baseline collaboration almost automatically. People using these tools are informed and able to share information instantly. Finally, and directly to my point, unadulterated collaboration works because by definition it connects us to each other.

Research shows that from a human standpoint, we perform best when we work together in small groups. Our brains are wired to focus on a limited number of relationships at a time.[11] We naturally congregate in small groups and collaborate with people we trust. The result: no matter who the organization chart says is in charge, more work gets done in collaborative groups. As organizations realize this, they will find ways to collaborate efficiently.[12]

Collaboration Killers

With all of its utility as a key component of emotional connect-edness, many times I still see attempts to collaborate that have the opposite effect—employee engagement takes a hit, and productiv-ity declines commensurately. Why? Collaboration gone wrong can be time-consuming, unpopular, costly, unfocused, and inefficient. No one likes to be "forced" to collaborate, nor does anyone like to submit to a change that only makes things worse. The so-called *collaboration paradox* (when working together yields weaker results)[13] is a negative by-product of several dysfunctional team dynamics.

The first, most pervasive barrier is a lack of trust. As the first of five dimensions in emotional connectedness, collaboration is arguably the element that is most dependent upon trust. It be-came clear to me based on my study that collaboration can con-nect people effectively only when individuals feel secure enough to innovate, share ideas, and offer advice without fear of reprisal. This core finding correlates with the noted two-year study conducted by Google in 2015, mentioned above, that looked at 250 attri-butes of Google teams and found that psychological safety was one of the main dynamics that set successful teams apart from other teams at Google. They found that the safer team members felt with one another, the more likely they were to admit mistakes, partner, and take on new roles.[14]

In my own collaborative experiences, I have seen that the deepest sharing occurs within groups where trust is a key com-ponent. For example, the BPI Talent Consortiums session I con-ducted in Lower Manhattan on the tenth anniversary of the 9/11 attacks, mentioned in the Introduction, is a case in point. The group opened up their hearts and described vulnerable moments in their lives to each other and what they learned. A key compo-nent of that session? Establishing a bond based on trust. We spent the first part of the day laying out ironclad ground rules, discussing the common experiences that brought us together, and creating a level playing field where everyone agreed to participate and respect opposing feelings and perspectives.

Indeed, psychological safety frees us up to contribute fully and openly. Harvard professor Amy Edmondson, who coined the term "psychological safety" in research she published in 1999, has said that it brings about "a sense of confidence that the team will not embarrass, reject, or punish someone for speaking up."[15] With psychological safety comes not only trust but also inclusion and diversity, as more of us are willing to be fully present in groups and express diverse perspectives. Without psychological safety, and all that it yields within teams, attempts to collaborate will fail every time.

A second barrier to collaboration is weak or inexperienced leadership. On the one hand, this includes leaders who are unable or unwilling to delegate. Control-obsessed leaders struggle to exhibit emotional intelligence, sometimes to the point of being pathologically opposed to including others in the process or considering an opposing argument.

Deborah Lipman Slobodnik, my mentor and a noted executive coach and expert in team leadership and culture change, told me: "One of the big killers of collaboration is leaders who are only going through the motions in terms of creating an inclusive process," she said. "They say they want to hear from their peers, but they have already made up their mind, and usually the entire team knows that." The effect is a team that is demoralized and disillusioned.[16]

The flip side of this negative scenario, on the other hand, is leaders who fail to communicate the rules and who neglect to set up a team structure or clarify decision rights. Lack of proper process leads to drawn-out debates, endless meetings, lack of closure, and the hopeless quest for consensus. At a minimum, team members need to know the purpose of the team, the roles and responsibilities of the people on the team, and how decisions are made. Some organizations have formal team guidelines to clarify structure and settle disputes; others have informal mentors or advisors who can share best practices. No matter how it's accomplished, teams need enough structure to remain on track and get things done.

The final barrier to collaboration I will mention is political maneuvering, bullying, and similar bad behavior created by abusing unequal power dynamics. Tom Kolditz, retired brigadier general and head of behavioral science and leadership at West Point, told me about team dysfunction in the theater of combat training during his work with U.S. and South Korean soldiers in South Korea in the late 1990s.

At the time, Kolditz was leading an organization of about 800 people, including 100 South Korean soldiers assigned to train with the U.S. forces. The South Korean soldiers, he said, were "super bright and extremely good with computers and automation. And every one of them was a black belt in Taekwondo. But they didn't enjoy high social status compared to the U.S. soldiers."[17] The South Koreans were in the minority in the unit, and the U.S. forces tended to be more physically fit and heavily muscled, both of which are important in an artillery unit. The result, Kolditz told me, was that the South Koreans were systematically marginalized and ridiculed.

"When you've got different types of people working in an organization, it's pretty easy for cliques and barriers to get thrown up," he said. "But it's clearly dysfunctional, and on a team of this nature it can be catastrophic."

Kolditz addressed the situation by creating a more even power dynamic.

"I required certain segments of training to be conducted in the native Korean language. It changed things by making American soldiers completely dependent on the Koreans. Suddenly, the Korean soldiers became the top commodity in every one of my hundred-person subunits," he said. The result? "Over a span of about two or three months, they went from being second-class citizens in a dysfunctional relationship with the U.S. soldiers to being really close, cohesive members of that team."

While combat training on foreign soil with multiple nationalities expected to collaborate is team training to the extreme, politics and power dynamics can create a disruptive, dysfunctional situation in any environment. Kolditz turned the tide by elevating the status of the individuals who were being treated as outsiders. He also instituted a "zero tolerance policy for disrespecting people on the team and their abilities." These are the same types of policies and training norms that organizations create to avoid bullying, harassment, and discrimination.

As with other "rules of the road" for collaboration, respect needs to be explicit, enforced, and modeled from the top down. As we will see in the Best Practices Playbook below, coaxing the magic from collaboration is about balancing structure and flexibility, and it's about giving people guidelines but allowing them to learn from the mistakes they make.

Systemic Collaboration: The Best Practices Playbook

Collaborating in a way that keeps people connected may seem a little like harnessing alchemy. It is impossible to fully predict what combination of players will produce the creative spark to make collaboration great, but you need some science or structure to protect people from unexpected outcomes. This balancing act gives you the latitude to improvise, even as it calls for an effective game plan.

Atlassian, the Australian enterprise software firm that makes collaboration tools, is an example of a company that seems to have struck the right balance within its own workforce. It gives employees a large dose of freedom and independence by virtue of its flat management structure and team-of-teams approach, and its core values include "the courage and resourcefulness to spark change." Yet, it also provides employees with a video playbook to help steer teams to solve problems, forge forward, and operate according to Atlassian's high-achievement, ultra-collaborative culture.

In a recent interview, Atlassian's cofounder and CEO suggested that maintaining the company's culture comes down to hiring people you trust and setting the right priorities, including "making sure people know experimentation is important, making sure they know the bounds of the strategy and the company, what's acceptable and not acceptable."[18]

In my research, as well as in my everyday work coaching executives, I have seen that this combination of freedom and control enables collaboration when these guiding principles, discussed below, are put into practice across the company (Figure 3.1).

FIGURE 3.1

1. Equal Airtime

In the beginning of Barack Obama's first term as president, the majority of the top White House staffers were men who had worked on the campaign. Female aides were outnumbered, and their voices were drowned out in important policy discussions. When they tried to get a word in, their ideas were talked over or hijacked. Ultimately, the female staffers solved their problem by adopting a strategy they called "amplification." When one woman in their group made a key point, another woman would repeat it, emphasizing the idea and giving credit to its author. Their tactic forced the men in the room to listen up and give everyone equal airtime.[19]

These female power brokers managed to solve their own problem by supporting each other, but the example also goes to show that dysfunction can manifest in any group and at any level. Social scientists agree that diverse teams yield greater creativity and output than homogeneous teams—but only if everyone has a chance to participate. Interestingly, I've found people feel they are In Great Company when they are afforded a chance to speak up. They feel emotionally connected to each other when their voices are heard, even when their perspective is not always heeded.

In an interview, Helen Russell, chief people officer at Atlassian, succinctly explained how equal airtime yields emotional connectedness within their culture: "At the beginning of each executive meeting [at Atlassian], everyone has the mic for two minutes, and we each have a minute to say what's top of mind from a personal perspective and a minute on what's top of mind from a business perspective. Since we started this practice, it is unbelievable what I've discovered about my peers. You just have no clue what's going on in your colleagues' lives until that moment when they disclose things. It evokes a completely different level of empathy and connection. Having those moments to just situate what's going on with colleagues enables us all to be more trusting and to interact from a more humane and empathetic point of view."[20]

As simple as it sounds, equal airtime requires setting corporate politics aside and adopting norms that enable equal sharing of ideas with no tolerance for monopolizing discussions. The practices mentioned below signal respect for all and create a work environment where people feel safe taking risks and thinking creatively.

Make Equal Airtime a Management Priority

Like many things, leaders set the tone for how collaboration occurs. For instance, Atlassian's custom of giving every person time to talk at the outset of executive meetings is likely to spill over into how all of their teams interact.

Leaders can send the message in numerous ways, but the best option is to model open, inclusive behavior and make collaboration more about ideas and implementation and less about grandstanding and deferring to job title.

Address the Collaboration Killers

There are three team archetypes that need to be neutralized in order to create an atmosphere of equal airtime. The first, the *Steamrollers*, are the people who hijack a team discussion. They proceed with their ideas in a single-minded manner without pausing to include others or yielding to objections, questions, or comments. Oftentimes, Steamrollers get a lot accomplished quickly, but their progress is detrimental to the larger group dynamic.

The next archetype, the *Alpha Bullies*, make a habit of intimidating or marginalizing colleagues. They show little respect for others in the group, particularly those they deem to be weak, and the net effect is that collaboration comes to a halt when psychological safety breaks down.

The third archetype, the *Slackers*, sit back and let other people do the difficult work of debating ideas, options, and solutions. They have little to add because either they are disengaged, or they have not done the requisite preparation.

Establishing ground rules can eliminate some of these collaboration killers, but that's not enough. Equal airtime is just one positive by-product of having a culture that is open and inclusive. When that culture is in place, these archetypes either opt out or are weeded out to make room for people whose values are aligned with the organization.

Use an Icebreaker

The immense benefits of equal airtime—including better ideas and more creative solutions—only materialize when people actually participate. Even when collaboration killers are neutralized, not everyone is willing to express themselves. Whether it is because they are extremely reserved or because they don't feel safe interjecting themselves, they may need some extra encouragement. This is often the case when a cross-functional team is first formed and some members outrank others in terms of job title or hierarchy.

One tactic to change the dynamic is to ask an open-ended question that everyone can answer. Another is to respectfully call on people who don't volunteer, thereby demonstrating that you are genuinely interested in their perspective. Or you can plan opportunities to socialize and get to know each other, to create camaraderie and elevate everyone's comfort level. These and other icebreakers knock down emotional barriers between people and start to create connections.

Ensure a Balance of Team Roles

Teams can veer out of control when there is not a balance of power. My mentor, Deborah Lipman Slobodnik, taught me about the four players in a team who are essential for coming to a decision and executing effectively. Too much of any role (or the absence of it) creates an imbalance of power.

The first role is the *Challenger*. Challengers question an existing thought or idea. They may say things like, "What brings you to that conclusion? I ask because I don't see it that way. I see it this way."

The next role is the *Supporter*. Typically, Supporters agree, lend their credibility, and thus give the idea more staying power. They also provide a "vote" for a person's idea.

The third role is the *Mirror*. The Mirrors restate what they think they have heard until the individual stating the idea agrees with the Mirrors' interpretation. The Mirrors are essential because they bring the idea into clarity for the rest of the group.

The last role is the *Mover*. The Movers take the thinking of the group to the next practical level—it is where execution occurs.

Imagine a group with not enough or too many people in any one of these roles. Sound frustrating or familiar?

Maintain Focus

There's a reason that not every group can abide by an equal airtime policy: because it can easily yield unintended consequences and lead to rambling diatribes or off-topic remarks that eat up time. (It's no wonder people are cynical about collaboration.)

The key to keeping collaboration on track is making sure everyone is aligned around a common objective. With that, it is easier to assign roles and create accountability for maintaining focus during the exchange of ideas. This is made easier through any number of collaboration tools that help people remain on track when they are communicating in person or through an online platform or social network.

2. Mindful Listening

Mindful listening is inextricably linked to equal airtime. *In fact, some might argue that listening is even more critical than speaking when it comes to enjoying the benefits of collaboration and sparking an emotional connection.*

I saw this dynamic play out with executives at KeyBank as part of their merger with First Niagara Group in 2015. At the time, KeyBank's chief talent officer, Brian Fishel, who was charged with leading the integration process, was fully cognizant that mergers fail to meet their goals a full 83 percent of the time—and he was determined to beat the odds.[21]

Unlike so many other mergers I've seen, Fishel was heavily focused on using effective listening to bridge the cultures of the two companies. As part of that, he developed a robust game plan that included onboarding and training sessions, bringing leaders from both organizations together to listen to each other's concerns and talk through their practices and values. Through these sessions, executives on both sides learned that they shared many of the same foundational elements or "enterprise DNA"—which, research suggests, is rarely the case in merger-acquisitions. These core elements, including organizational norms, highlighted strong similarities and created a genuine bond between the leaders at both banks. These listening and learning sessions were well attended and ultimately paved the way for the success of the merger.

Research corroborates the notion that effective listening improves collaboration. For instance, one study from 2018 paired student public speakers with either attentive, respectful listeners or distracted, disengaged listeners.[22] The researchers found that the speakers who were paired with attentive listeners were "less anxious, more self-aware, and reported higher clarity about their attitudes on the topics" compared to those paired with distracted listeners.[23] The researchers also found that "speakers who conversed with a good listener reported attitudes that were more complex and less extreme—in other words, not one-sided."[24]

Just as effective listening strengthens the bond between speaker and listener, listening is likewise a key to collaborative efforts with these prescriptive strategies as pillars for success.

Be Fully Present

When I coach executives about how to be mindful listeners, I often begin with their eyes, not their ears. Getting started with effective listening actually starts with training your gaze on the speaker, assuming the speaker is within sight. In other words, put your phone down and focus.

Other elemental items to put into practice for effective listening? Remain mindful. Paying attention, focusing on what the person is saying, and keeping an open mind are not things that most of us do automatically. Finally, pause to make sure you know the other person is finished talking before you speak up or respond. The bottom line is that effective listening requires conscious effort.

Take a Listening Tour

When KeyBank's Brian Fishel brought people together to listen following the merger with First Niagara, he was on to something powerful. Top leaders and employees gained key insights based on what they heard. Other leaders have benefited by making similar moves. In his first year as Canada's prime minister, for instance, Justin Trudeau took a listening tour, meeting everyday people in restaurants, hockey rinks, and town halls across the country.

Similarly, when David Abney joined UPS as its CEO in 2014, one of the first things he did was go on a worldwide listening tour to hear what UPS employees had to say.[25] As these cases show, listening tours by leaders and executives are especially effective during times of transition: following a merger, change in leadership, or a strategy shift. This is arguably when leaders can best benefit from hearing a broad range of ideas. In addition, the act of listening gives employees a chance to be heard at a time when anxiety levels are especially high.

Yet, a listening tour is only effective if it is a genuine effort. Leaders need to really listen, consider the content, and make decisions that reflect what they have heard.

Defer Judgment

We all come to collaborations with our own agendas, experiences, and preconceived notions. But effective listening requires us to set these items aside. We need to listen to understand what the other person is saying, as opposed to using our energy to formulate our rebuttal.

The secret to deferring judgment is twofold. First, reflect on the content of what the other person is saying. Don't listen to *decide*. Listen to understand the speaker's message and perspective. Second, and perhaps less known, is to reflect on your own feelings and reactions as they occur. You can neutralize your trigger-based responses by understanding what is driving your emotions and setting them aside with the intention of mindful listening.

Engage with Empathy

In my work coaching executives and teams, I have found that empathy is a core ingredient of effective listening. Although empathy can be practiced through conscious effort, it should begin by having an authentic interest in what the other person has to say.

Why bother adding empathy to your mode of listening? Empathetic listeners achieve a deeper understanding of what the speaker is saying, thereby making collaboration easier. But there is another important perk: empathy creates emotional connectedness. Almost by definition, empathetic listening helps you identify with the speaker, which creates an emotional bond based on shared understanding.

3. Free Flow of Information

In most organizations, knowledge is a currency that either drives collaboration forward and enriches it or stops it in its tracks. Knowledge sharing and open communication are tremendous drivers of value in collaborative endeavors.

At Atlassian, for example, "openness" is a core value that keeps people connected to the company. Their mantra is "open company, no bullshit," and they express it like this in their internal conversations and recruiting materials: "Openness is root level for us. Information is open internally by default, and sharing is a first principle. And we understand that speaking your mind requires equal parts brains (what to say), thoughtfulness (when to say it), and caring (how it's said)."[26]

In a blog by Atlassian CEO Mike Cannon-Brookes, he said that on high-performing teams, "information flows freely and team members have access to the resources they need to get work done. These teams work 'open.'" He went on to write that openness defines the most impactful teams along three dimensions: "Open ways of working, open ways of thinking, and open ways of being."[27] As part of that, Atlassian shares financial data openly with employees and encourages them to respectfully challenge the status quo.[28]

This open ethos seems to be working for Atlassian. Total revenue at the highly collaborative company was $174.3 million for the fourth quarter of fiscal 2017, up 37 percent from $127.6 million for the fourth quarter of fiscal 2016.[29]

Yet, not all companies have mastered this open dynamic, and often knowledge is hoarded for personal prestige or political gain. Creating the right incentives and structure can go a long way to encouraging everyone to contribute and share knowledge and ideas openly.

These are the best practices I have seen firsthand as part of my work with organizations to create a culture of openness and emotional connection.

Incentivize Information Sharing

The secrets to success are creating ground rules that incentivize knowledge sharing instead of knowledge hoarding and building a culture where open communication is expected and valued. Nonmonetary incentives include things like respect, recognition, and leadership. Respect, for one, is an organic incentive for knowledge sharing. Yet, for respect to truly bear fruit as an incentive, the organizational culture must also actively model a corresponding intolerance for knowledge hoarding. If keeping knowledge to oneself is adequately deterred, then the choice to share it becomes almost automatic.

Recognition, as well, can be a naturally occurring incentive for knowledge sharing that takes many shapes. Organizations can recognize sharing (of ideas or information) informally, by giving people a shout-out for their efforts, or formally with a letter of recognition from a member of the leadership team. One organization I know has a "recognition toolkit," whereby employees add new ideas for ways to recognize each other. Regardless of how you choose to do it, building recognition around knowledge sharing can serve as a strong incentive.

Finally, a position of leadership within the group is perhaps the most powerful nonfinancial incentive for knowledge sharing. Although power dynamics need to maintain an equilibrium that benefits the whole group, rotating leadership based on ideas and insights can be one part of encouraging members to share their knowledge.

Work Across Functions

Eliminating silos and working across functions encourages knowledge sharing for a few reasons. First, cross-functional teams are made up of individuals with varying types of expertise. This elimination of overlap leads to less competition, making it easier for people to swap diverse perspectives. Next, breaking down silos creates a norm where resources—including information—need to be shared as a matter of course in order for the team to perform. Finally, leaders of teams or cross-functional units are typically expected to incentivize members to share knowledge.

Even so, many experts would argue that breaking down traditional departmental silos and reorganizing across functions can create a new type of silo—where new barriers are built between competing teams. To avoid this effect, make sure each team has a clear and distinct objective. The other, and perhaps greatest, way to eliminate the silo effect is to build a culture that values collaboration and the open sharing of information.

Focus on the Magic Middle

When we focus on collaboration, we tend to zero in on perfecting dynamics among team members. Yet, the bottleneck in information sharing often occurs in middle management, where knowledge is more likely to be held or hoarded.

With a collaborative team approach, middle managers may feel their authority being threatened, as power is evenly distributed across the organization with individuals making decisions for themselves. More than anything else, this presents a training opportunity. Middle managers who are accustomed to *managing* information can learn to shift their focus to effectively distributing information and eliminating friction in the knowledge network.

Extend the Openness to the Outside

Many companies that value transparency have found that the upside of openness extends beyond their corporate walls. Public companies have requirements to provide public information about financial performance and business practices, but today customers expect far greater transparency and constant communication about everything from corporate values to everyday business.

Although companies should set their own ground rules about how (and how much) information is shared publicly online and through social channels, the most collaborative firms share information and solicit feedback in return from customers and stakeholders. Companies like Zappos, for example, tap into their connections to customers, and the information that flows back to the company is utilized to make decisions about product development. This collaborative approach, which includes customers and suppliers, adds a rich dimension to openness and transparency, and it sends a signal to employees about the importance of sharing knowledge for the purpose of collaboration.

4. Mix of Structure and Flexibility

Collaboration's sweet spot exists at the intersection of structure and flexibility. *My research for In Great Company reveals that we need to organize individuals to succeed by having guardrails in place, but we also need to allow enough free rein to leverage creative instincts and agility.* I mentioned Atlassian, where teams operate in the flow with relative freedom and fluidity, equipped with the guidelines in the company's Team Playbook. The playbook, which contains many levels of resources, from checklists and videos to team health diagnostics, offers ideas for keeping teams balanced, making difficult decisions, and containing conflicts before they erupt.[30] The playbook works for Atlassian because it offers collaborators the right mix of structure and flexibility. The playbook has become so popular that in 2016 Atlassian made it publicly available online and urged other companies to use it to improve their own collaborative efforts.

Another, much larger organization that has focused on how to structure for collaboration is General Motors. Michael Arena, chief talent officer at GM, told me about their work tapping into employee networks by leveraging the power of connectivity and relationships.[31] The point is to "identify innovators within the organization and position them to connect with others and do their best work together." This nuanced approach looks beyond a typical hierarchical structure to create a superstructure based on "social capital."

"We can hire really bright people, but if we can't get them positioned effectively, in such a way where they can have an impact, they're useless," Arena said. "Then it's just un-seized potential sitting on the margins of the organization."[32]

Both GM and Atlassian are creating structures that have flexibility embedded in them, allowing people to adapt to change, respond to opportunities faster, and connect and collaborate more effectively. This syncs up with several of the five dimensions of emotional connectedness, but it nests most neatly within collaboration because it corroborates several important prescriptions, as follows.

Combine Freedom and Focus

Spotify and ING organize according to the Agile development model of "Squads, Tribes, and Chapters." W.L. Gore, maker of

Gor-tex fabric, blends culture with structure to organize as a "latticework of strong interconnected talents woven together like a tapestry."[33]

Digital enterprises like Airbnb and Zappos have experimented with the idea of Holocracy, which eliminates traditional leaders and empowers decision-making at the individual level. While it's clear that these particular organizing structures are not for every company, collaboration works best when the structure allows the combination of freedom and focus mentioned above. Just as collaboration should add flexibility to an organization, any structure today should deliver the agility to keep businesses competitive and engage employees.

Use the Power of People

Studies show that "the burden of collaboration in organizations is unevenly distributed," with "20 to 35 percent of value-added collaborations coming from only 3 to 5 percent of employees."[34] This tells us that we need to identify the most talented collaborators among us and support and reward them accordingly. This is exactly what Michael Arena is exploring within GM. Based on in-depth research by Rob Cross and Wayne Baker[35] on the topic of "mapping energy in social networks," Arena is identifying Energizers— individuals who can spark progress on projects, evangelize ideas, and attract others to join the cause.

"We're identifying them, partnering with them, and incorporating them in the design process," Arena said.

This practice of mapping and tapping into the social network inside large complex organizations allows organizations like GM to support not only the Energizers who diffuse energy across their network but also several other important network archetypes vital to the collaboration. Active and deliberate, knowing who your most powerful collaborators are enables you to recognize their work and pave the way for others to join and support them.

Build Accountability into Collaboration

Empowering collaborators and relying on networks of interactions does not mean that people are not held accountable for results. *In teams, transparent goals and accountability expectations should be baked right into the structure. Team leaders and members need to hold each other accountable.*

The other key element in accountability is feedback. Part of the promise of collaboration is the ability of teams to place small bets, experiment, and course correct based on what they learn.

5. Conflict Resolution

Fueled by diverse thinking and varied perspectives, collaboration creates emotional connectedness when differences can be leveraged to create connections, as opposed to sowing divisiveness and discord.

Perhaps the thorniest of the five positive best practices for collaboration, I learned the most about consensus building from Senator George Mitchell.[36] Not only a U.S. senator and Senate majority leader, Mitchell was also the principal architect of the Good Friday [Peace] Agreement in Northern Ireland, and U.S. special envoy for Middle East peace (2009 to 2011). His historic experience, rounded out by work on corporate boards including Disney, Xerox, and FedEx, points to several themes to consider as we examine collaboration.

First, he said, consensus building requires a strong belief in a fair process.

"You can't always get everyone to agree," he said. "But by conducting yourself properly, you can get everyone to agree that the process by which a decision was reached was fair and open." With that, Mitchell said, all sides may abide by the outcome because they feel that it was decided upon properly with impartial rules of order.

Next, Mitchell said, consensus building requires rising above interpersonal differences that would only serve to deepen the conflict. "The lesson for me was that it is possible to play a constructive role in ending conflict without directly engaging in the conflict ourselves," he said. As part of that, Mitchell said that remaining above the fray requires patience and dedication to the cause of conflict resolution.

Finally, Mitchell said, groups must remain focused on finding a solution. In Northern Ireland, he said, the United States helped bring about an end to a conflict that had gone on for decades "without firing a single bullet or spending any money, because we led by example and had a president [Bill Clinton] who was tenacious in persevering, despite repeated setbacks, and despite the unwillingness of any of his predecessors to directly involve themselves in efforts to end the conflict."

While the stakes were arguably much higher for Mitchell and the United States than they will be in our own collaborative efforts in companies, many of the same lessons apply: agree on a fair and consistent process, rise above personal differences, and remain committed to finding a solution. Here's how they translate in situations in which individuals need to collaborate in an everyday setting.

Don't Skip Steps

As Mitchell said, just as conflict resolution requires considerable patience, it is important to recognize that getting buy-in as part of collaboration is a process. According to Deborah Slobodnik, this process is more like a conversation with two parts. "There's the divergence, where you get to brainstorm and sell your viewpoint," she said. "But then you have to be able to turn the corner and get to convergence." This convergence, she said, goes beyond making a decision to achieving buy-in and support for the decision.

Whether your process is 2 steps or 10, it's important that people know it and feel that is it is being used consistently and fairly.

Neutralize the Negative

Keeping conflicts under control to accelerate collaboration requires staunching negativity. Sometimes that may mean something basic, like keeping the discourse respectful as a matter of course, while other times it may require training leaders in the art and science of conflict resolution.

Chris Voss, former lead hostage negotiator for the FBI and the author of *Never Split the Difference*, suggests diffusing difficult interactions by addressing negative emotions first, and then moving on to say something positive. "This intentional sequence is the complete opposite of what everybody is taught, and opposite of human nature. We're taught to go after the positives initially to set things up right," he said. "But negative emotions present barriers that are formidable, and you actually you need to go after them first to have a positive outcome."[37]

Similarly, he suggests labeling negative feelings, showing that you understand where they come from, and making an empathetic statement. Examples of empathetic statements that take negative feelings into account include these: "It seems like you feel that this is unfair," or "I am hearing that I am not taking your interests into account." According to neuroscience, Voss has said, identifying or labeling a negatives emotion diffuses it without agreeing or disagreeing to what the person is thinking or feeling.

Taking Voss's sage advice for neutralizing negativity is a strategy that requires us to be prepared. At the very least, to deliver a hit of dopamine or serotonin in this way, we need to observe and understand other people's negative feelings and carefully manage our own.

Get Beyond Consensus

In my research, I heard that people felt In Great Company when collaboration yielded a total that was greater than the sum of its parts. In the context of managing conflicts in groups, that means going beyond consensus to turn differences in opinion into something powerful and positive.

To accept the inevitability of conflict and take collaboration to the next level, we need to go back to psychological safety and ensure that we have created a safe place to engage—to explore diverse, and even opposing, perspectives until the end result is a meaningfully better combination or a new solution altogether.

• • •

Collaboration is just one element of EC, but it is critical because without it, the other elements fall apart. There is no values alignment or respect, for instance, without collaboration. And we need all five pieces of the EC puzzle to truly be In Great Company.

SYSTEMIC COLLABORATION: EXECUTIVE SUMMARY

Positive Best Practices	Ground Rules
Equal airtime	Make equal airtime a management priority. Address the collaboration killers. Use an icebreaker. Ensure a balance of team roles. Maintain focus.
Mindful listening	Be fully present. Take a listening tour. Defer judgment. Engage with empathy.
Free flow of information	Incentivize information sharing. Work across functions. Focus on the magic middle. Extend the openness to the outside.
Mix of structure and flexibility	Combine freedom and focus. Use the power of people. Build accountability into collaboration.
Conflict resolution	Don't skip steps. Neutralize the negative. Get beyond consensus.

CHAPTER 4

POSITIVE FUTURE

At the grand opening of Big River Steel in 2014, a masked figure—larger than life—dressed in all black leather and a black helmet rode up to the plant in Osceola, Arkansas, on a hulking Harley-Davidson motorcycle made of blazing steel. The bike made its way in and up to a stage, where the stunt double who was driving slipped off into the wings as Mark Bula, who was Big River's chief commercial officer at the time, strode on stage for the launch event, clad in all black leather and carrying a helmet. It was a striking moment marked with open excitement, and it was symbolic of the culture Big River leaders were trying to create. A culture where people would be passionate enough about steel to break the mold and do things differently.

"Thinking about that day still gives me the chills," Bula tells me. "It sent an unmistakable message to our employees: we were there to throw out the status quo."

Big River Steel is a tech company that just happens to make steel. Located in an area of Arkansas that company insiders call "steel mill heaven" (based on its proximity to the Mississippi River on the east and a major railroad line and interstate on the west),

Big River is rethinking what it means to make steel. As part of that, Bula told me they take an entrepreneurial approach to American manufacturing.[1] In order to live into their promise as a steel innovator, he said, they "attract and train the best technicians in the business and equip them with the most advanced technology."

By all accounts, Big River Steel has many of the ingredients that define the positive future element of being In Great Company.

First, Big River is highly *innovative*. Arguably one of the most technologically advanced scrap recycling and steel production facilities in the world, it is also the first "Flex Mill."[2] The company trademarked the term to describe its innovative capability to employ high-tech equipment and highly skilled workers to "flex" and produce steel for a range of industries and uses, from highly specialized automotive products and railcars to energy products and infrastructure projects.

Next, it stands for *individual empowerment*. As part of their inception, Big River spent over $10 million on training to set their people up for success. Bula said the leadership team believes in "empowering the workforce so they feel comfortable carving their role in the company and developing whom they become as individuals." He summed it up like this: "By design, it is in our DNA to want to challenge existing assumptions about the industry. As part of that, we encourage our people to have a 'rebel mentality' so that collectively we can put the status quo aside and be the best at what we do."

Finally, the organization is *future oriented*. The company invested $1.3 billion to build a facility that is Leadership in Energy and Environmental Design (LEED) certified, which is a rating system designed to track environmental performance of a building and encourage sustainability. In addition, the Big River plant is a model for the utilization of artificial intelligence. The company partnered with a San Francisco–based start-up to install thousands of sensors that deliver next-generation data to help them become the first smart steel production facility, equipped to monitor and improve maintenance planning, production line scheduling, logistics operations, safety, and environmental protection.

All of this adds up to an adaptable, fast-moving organization where people feel energized and engaged to act independently and perform at their peak.

We define the positive future element of In Great Company broadly, as having a forward-facing outlook, a powerful vision for the future, and a capacity for innovative execution. *In my study, I found that people feel emotionally connected when an organization has a specific vision for success; processes and a philosophy that set people up to contribute; and the opportunity to play a role in meaningful progress and positive transformation.* Oftentimes, the organizations that score highest in their EC scores for positive future are the innovative, entrepreneurial organizations that have a plan to become industry leaders by investing in their people, enabling experimentation, and driving forward toward an exciting future.

Why a Positive Future Keeps Us Connected

The building blocks of positive future—positive future outlook, progress, and innovation—help create and sustain engagement in the workplace. While they each make up important parts of this element of EC, the first of the three, positive future outlook, has the deepest roots in academic work as a subset of the vibrant positive psychology movement.

The term *positive psychology* first appeared in a 1954 book by psychologist Abraham Maslow.[3] Yet, the modern positive psychology movement itself started more recently. Most agree it became a new area of study and practice in 1998, when well-known psychologist and author Martin Seligman selected it as the main theme for his term as president of the American Psychological Association.[4]

Along with the two main codevelopers of positive psychology, Hungarian-American psychologist Mihaly Csikszentmihalyi and the late Christopher Peterson, psychologist and professor at University of Michigan, Seligman's work was widely distributed through positive psychology research centers on understanding and cultivating individual well-being and happiness, including what makes us flourish as humans. The area of study and the body of published research are vast, and positive psychology clearly shows that a positive outlook improves our health and happiness.[5]

While positive future as it relates to my work on emotional connectedness is not entirely aligned with positive psychology in terms of the range of concepts it covers, there is clear and significant overlap inasmuch as both relate to how a positive orientation by employees, and the degree to which an organization is set up to encourage it, creates a sense of belonging and engagement among and between people at work.

The next building block of positivity—progress—is another established driver of employee engagement and satisfaction. A study by Harvard Business School professor Teresa Amabile and psychologist Steven Kramer, for example, found that the happiest and most productive days for people at work were those marked by forward momentum and a sense of progress.[6] Amabile and Kramer argue that the power of progress is fundamental to human nature, and it is a primary ingredient in motivation.[7] Ample additional studies show that our ability to achieve progress is a critical key to happiness, plain and simple.

Csikszentmihalyi's more recent work on "flow" further serves to connect progress and happiness. According to Csikszentmihalyi, "The best moments in our lives are not the passive, receptive, relaxing times. . . . The best moments usually occur if a person's body or mind is stretched to its limits in a voluntary effort to accomplish something difficult and worthwhile." These "best moments" are what Csikszentmihalyi calls *flow*, and he says it is an important contributor to positive outlook and well-being.[8]

That syncs up with what I have found—that progress aligns and engages people and connects them to a common purpose.

The last building block of positive future is innovation. Innovation is inextricably linked to both progress and positive outlook. Although it is a core concept of EC in its own right, the individuals in my study reported that the degree to which their organizations enabled innovation was an indication that they were disposed to encourage a positive outlook and enable progress. Other research supports this. For instance, one study of over 800 financial services employees found that a quarter of respondents wanted to move into the tech sector. Why? In part because they believed they would find working for an innovative organization to be more meaningful.[9]

In general, positive future creates cohesiveness and social connection. By delivering upbeat emotions and happiness, it changes our brain chemistry, making us feel safe, supported, and able to push for progress in the workplace.

Breaking down Barriers to Positive Future

With positive future being so, well, positive, why is it such an outlier in the workplace? Like everything else, it's complicated.

As part of my work with organizations, I consult with leaders to conduct culture interventions to help turn around engagement and performance when a workplace becomes toxic, demoralized, or otherwise negative in nature. This is an important subset of creating emotional connectedness because negative cultures repel people and destroy trust. As part of that work, I have found that the source of negativity can be either systemic or individual.

An example of a systemic source of negativity is business-as-usual practices such as micromanagement, red tape, and rigid systems that force us to settle for less. They can kill progress with a thousand cuts. According to Chris Voss, author and former FBI hostage negotiator, one of the biggest cuts is too much compromise. Compromise dilutes passion. Voss sums it up in one phrase: "never split the difference."[10]

"There's an old phrase that says a camel is a horse designed by committee. Well, that's compromise," Voss said. "Whatever kind of job you're trying to get done, no one is going to be satisfied by fitting two things together just to see what happens."

With compromise, everyone feels a little deflated. Voss has said that a better tool for creating a positive, future-focused work environment is collaboration. The process of collaboration includes taking diverse perspectives to arrive at the best solution. Ideally, Voss said, the team can use the power of passion to create a new solution that everyone owns.

Compromise or not, systemic negativity can manifest naturally based on how an organization is organized. Traditional companies tend to rely on strict hierarchy, for instance. With this, perks such as promotions, prestige, and pay increases are commensurate with one's position on the corporate ladder. Unless managed with vigilance, the result can be dysfunctional behavior including blame games, information hoarding, and passing the buck.

A similarly negative potential by-product of hierarchy gone wrong is fiefdoms that form based on corporate politics. In a number of organizations where I've consulted, for example, employees felt obligated, based on their reporting structure, to align with specific executives over the mission of the organization. The results were an environment where loyalty directed at leaders was rewarded over results and a situation where people told executives what they wanted to hear as opposed to what they really believed to be true.

Even flat or matrixed organizations can fall victim to this type of negative behavior if a company centralizes decision-making in the hands of a toxic leader, stifles transparency, or fails to genuinely empower people to do their job. When employees feel trapped in a system in which they can't be their best selves, negativity becomes a core part of the culture.

The other source of negativity in organizations is individual malfeasance. In some cases, hangers-on are allowed to remain and infect others with their vocal discontent. Whether you call them "loafers," "lifers," or just "habitual underperformers," when people fail to pull their weight or worse, intentionally dragging others down to their level, engagement and morale suffer. Similarly, individual negativity can likewise be the result of more than just a few bad apples. For instance, negativity can manifest when individuals at all levels get stuck in their ways and are allowed to resist change and repel innovation. Individual negativity can even cascade from the top down, when a toxic leader habitually fails to recognize positive contributions, yet fixates on failure and magnifies mistakes. In this case, direct reports become afraid to take appropriate risks, and everyone gets stuck in status quo behavior.

Regardless of the source, systemic and individual negativity can cripple an organization and make it impossible to recruit and retain high-performing individuals. The antidote to both systemic and individual negativity is to implement a set of carefully cultivated best practices, mentioned below, that create emotional connectedness and help create and sustain a positive future.

Positive Future: The Best Practices Playbook

Among the many possible options for using a positive future vision to spark EC, open innovation is particularly apt because it brings many more people together to combine ideas and expertise. Perhaps the best example of an organization using *open innovation* to forge a positive future for themselves is NASA.

While the agency never failed to capture the imagination of the public, NASA's existence seemed in doubt after the International Space Station was completed and the Space Shuttle Program ended. These problems did not occur because NASA lacked future aspirations but because space exploration is extraordinarily expensive and NASA funding was increasingly being siphoned off to support other government programs. That's where open innovation came in. In order to fund Mars exploration and other initiatives, NASA crowdsourced resources from the private sector, made its own patent portfolio available to inventors and entrepreneurs, and partnered to tackle some of the most pressing items on its agenda. The most public partnership by NASA was their collaboration with SpaceX to develop rockets and launch cargo to the International Space Station. Even after NASA's $140 billion investment in the SpaceX partnership, one study found that the collaboration had created efficiencies within NASA, and it had saved the agency hundreds of millions of dollars.[11]

As it did for NASA, open innovation can open doors and bring many more minds together to share ideas and resources along the path to a positive future. But open innovation is just one possible play among many in the positive future playbook (Figure 4.1).

1. Leverage Passion

Big River's entire corporate culture was designed to steer employee and customer sentiment in a positive direction and prevail against massively challenging headwinds. The inevitable question that loomed around the launch in 2014 was: why start a new steel company? And the very best answer they had was: *because that's what rebels do*. They portrayed the organization as a team of mavericks.

FIGURE 4.1

And it worked. People got fired up by the message and Big River's new and innovative methodology for making steel. Company executives created a "Rebels Wanted" logo, and employees put it in their cars, stuck it on their lunch boxes, and hung it in their homes.

The type of passion that makes you put the company bumper sticker on your car yields much more than just good PR. Passion delivers positivity because it makes employees evangelists. Evangelism and passion are critical in start-ups because the barriers to entry are high, success rates are low, and people need to give their all every day just to keep the ship sailing. But passion is important for all companies every day. In fact, according to research from Michael Mankins at Bain & Company, an engaged employee is 44 percent more productive than merely a satisfied worker, but an employee who feels truly inspired is nearly 125 percent more productive than a satisfied one. In other words, companies that leverage the passion of their employees outperform the rest.[12]

Creating a rebel brand is one way to get people fired up to innovate and perform at their best. There are other strategies as well that organizations can use to funnel passion as an ingredient of positive future.

Let Purpose Drive Passion

People are far more likely to be passionate about work if they believe their actions are changing the world for the better. Yet, not all of us are employed by Doctors Without Borders or another organization driven entirely by social mission. Still, companies can harvest passion in employees in nearly any industry.

Big River Steel stoked passion in their people by focusing their corporate culture squarely on things that deliver meaning: positive change in manufacturing, high quality standards, sustainability, empowerment, and innovation. Other companies, from Starbucks to Salesforce, have charitable foundations dedicated to advancing causes from strengthening the community to addressing climate change.

This combination of commerce and commitment allows people to work on behalf of their favorite causes under the umbrella of their own organization. Another way to generate purpose-driven passion in any company is to provide employees with flexibility to donate their time and skills during the workday to social causes. This simple measure may mean they bring their passion back to work with them.

Turn Passion into Products

Perhaps the best way to leverage people's passion is to listen to them and take their suggestions seriously. Innovative organizations like Amazon make a habit of empowering people to pitch their plans and side projects. For instance, the blockbuster success Amazon Prime came about after an Amazon software engineer floated the idea through the company's digital suggestion box. The Chinese appliance maker Haier is another organization known to encourage employees to pursue the ideas they are passionate about. In their case, they recognize employees for their contribution by naming the new product after them once it is commercialized.[13]

Some companies offer employees financial rewards for their best new ideas, others recognize them with awards and validation. Regardless of how it happens, giving employees a venue in which to express and pursue their ideas keeps their passion alive and focused in a productive direction.

Let Passion Pivot

Another part of enabling people to pursue ideas with passion is creating space for them to learn. Not all of our passions are worth pursuing, after all. Intuit encourages their innovators to pull the plug themselves when an idea or experiment is not panning out and directs them to pivot based on what they have learned.[14]

Likewise, Amazon treats every idea like a "two-way door"—the person who is leading development can turn back if he or she decides it is not working.[15] The takeaway is to empower people to experiment, but encourage them to course correct quickly. *Turning negative dynamics like failure into something positive has a double benefit: it provides a way for employees to pursue their passion without fear and it creates a larger culture of positivity.*

Look for Passionate Persuaders

Creating a culture of *positivity* attracts passionate people, but the onus is on everyone to sustain that culture. The first step is hiring passionate people. Projecting your expectations helps job candidates opt out of the process if the upbeat culture does not suit their personality. Likewise, recruiters can use assessments and interview questions to identify people who would be passionate in their work.

Big River Steel made it perfectly clear in their logo—"Rebels Wanted"—that they were looking for people with spark to help them actively reinvent the steel industry. Slackers need not apply. *Passion and positivity need to extend beyond the product development team. Middle managers, line staff, customer service, and the C suite—it only takes a few disengaged people to create a bottleneck that stops passion it its tracks.* Executives at Big River set the tone—the top team was overtly passionate about their start-up mission.

Put Passion in Its Place

As critical as passion is to positivity and success, left unchecked and unfocused it can divert attention from more important matters. I use three questions to help direct passion appropriately. First, is passion aligned with the business? While projects based on passion may be a way to unlock innovation and new business, they also need to meet business requirements and fit within the organization's mission.

Next, are you solving a problem that matters to customers? Like many things in business, drawing a direct line to customers focuses energy in the right direction and keeps new ideas market driven. Finally, is this sustainable? Not every passion project should be a business. Companies need criteria to help people know what ideas to keep or kill. Without guidelines, passion can become distracting.

2. Turn Change into a Positive

Things can turn negative fast in organizations. When companies are not performing well financially, people point fingers and look for someone to blame. When surprise events and unexpected disruptions send shock waves through industries, companies seize up and go back to the basics. When a new leader arrives on the scene and changes the norms, many of us push back and resist. Fear of change is widespread. It causes us to feel threatened, and it casts us into primordial fight-or-flight mode. While this physiological response to change is natural, it makes it all the more difficult to create and sustain a culture of positivity.

In order to be In Great Company, we need to do much more than simply accept change. We need to learn to view change in a positive light. Only by deliberately building change into our positive vision of the future can we realistically expect to succeed and advance in today's world of permanent disruption. James Citrin, leader of Spencer Stuart's North American CEO Practice, put it this way: "We can't get away from the need to translate and wade through change. If CEOs do not have the ability to learn, if they think that they have all the answers, then they are, by definition, going to be wrong."[16]

Spencer Stuart, the executive search and leadership development consulting firm, believes that the ability to accept and manage change presents such a powerful advantage for leaders that they have developed a tool to test for it. The Executive Intelligence evaluation tests and measures a leader's ability to thrive in new, unfamiliar, and complex situations. "There's so much disruption, there's so much technology, and there are so many new industries that leaders know very little with certainty," Citrin said. "The ability to learn and take in new information, and actually apply it in smart ways, is a core capability of great CEOs today."

Agreed. Reinvention is a core capability for almost everyone right now in any personal or professional leadership capacity. Change management is one of the best tools we can use to create a culture of positivity that connects us to each other. In addition to being ever present, change is a lever that mobilizes action and draws us together—ideally to move toward a more positive future. In my work with organizations, I teach people to reframe change as an opportunity as opposed to a threat and to use it to advance as leaders in a number of ways we will examine below.

Neutralize the Pain of Change

Whether it is organizational or personal, change entails letting go of things that we care about, such as beliefs, norms, and traditions. To pave the way for this difficult work, we need to acknowledge the pain that is involved and salvage the psychological safety that allows people to engage.

Chris Voss has proposed making confrontational situations—like change—more manageable by labeling negative emotions. Verbalizing and naming negative feelings allows people to move forward feeling positive, he said. A good use of emotional labeling would be, "You sound hurt by the decision. It doesn't seem fair." This direct, empathetic observation, Voss said, recognizes people's feelings without judging them, and it helps defuse their negative emotions.

Another way to neutralize the pain of change is to celebrate the success of old norms before moving on to the new normal. Pausing to acknowledge accomplishments and recognize success takes some of the sting out of change efforts and helps win over the hearts and minds of change resisters. This is especially important where change occurs in enduring institutions like corporate culture, when one segment or demographic in the organization may be brought into existing traditions and another has already moved on.

No matter how it is accomplished, recognizing the pain of change can neutralize negative feelings and create emotional connectedness.

Get Positive with "Deviants"

One of the most ingenious and inspiring strategies for engaging in positive change comes from the *positive deviance movement.*[17] Based on the observation that within most communities there are people whose uncommon behaviors or strategies enable them to find better solutions than their peers to the same seemingly intractable problems, the positive deviance approach requires no outside resources or additional knowledge.[18]

Put into practice by the late Jerry Sternin and his wife Monique as part of their lifesaving work with Save the Children in Vietnam in the 1990s, positive deviance helped address the dire child malnutrition crisis that existed in the region at the time.[19] Observing that traditional supplemental feeding programs (implemented by indigenous and international development organizations) provided only temporary solutions, the Sternins led the effort to identify cases in which local *positive deviants* solved their own problem with special practices and strategies that could be widely shared. In this instance, the positive deviance paradigm showed that poor families with well-nourished children supplemented their diet with foods traditionally considered inappropriate for children (sweet potato greens, shrimp, and crabs), fed them four times daily instead of twice, and washed their hands before meals.

Part of the appeal of this approach is its simplicity and utility:

▶ **D**efine the problem and what the outcome of a successful program to address it would look like. (This is usually stated in terms of behavior or a state of being.)

▶ **D**etermine if there are individuals with the community who already exhibit the desired behavior (that is, identify the presence of "positive deviants").

▶ **D**iscover their uncommon practices or strategies that enable the positive deviants to succeed when their neighbors do not.

▶ **D**esign an intervention enabling others in the community to access and practice the positive deviant behaviors.

Positive deviance created and sustained positive change in Vietnam and elsewhere for the same reason it has worked within organizations such as Merck and Hewlett Packard: it uses existing resources, highlights solutions that are already working, and champions best practices from within the community as opposed to being imposed by outside forces.[20] Change that springs from within a community or organization, through a process of self-examination, is viewed more positively by individuals engaging in change and has a higher likelihood of acceptance.

Offer More Ways to Change

Organizations need to create opportunities for leaders to disrupt themselves, including how they think, work, and lead. After all, the more comfortable a leader becomes with change, the easier it will be to find a positive, effective way to drive it forward organizationally.

The auto industry presents a case in point. With "radical disruption" on its doorstep, General Motors chief talent officer Michael Arena launched GM2020, a grassroots initiative designed to enable employees to "positively disrupt the way they work."[21] The far-reaching program positions employees for change through a variety of programs from design thinking seminars to "co-labs"— teams working entrepreneurially to find innovative solutions to problems. The point is to keep GM's workforce engaging in positive change to allow the organization to "keep pace with start-ups."

AT&T is undergoing a similar talent transformation. The telecomm and mass media behemoth is in the middle of a massive retraining effort to reeducate 100,000 employees and arm them with cutting-edge skills. In this case, the change effort is aimed at preparing employees for the future and creating the kind of nimble workforce the company needs to compete in the twenty-first century.[22]

Offering programs and training that incentivize employees to engage in change is yet another positive step to help them work together to prepare for the future.

3. Create Space to Innovate

Big River's CEO, Dave Stickler, loves to say: "We have one swear word around here that we aren't allowed to use, and that is: 'that's the way we've always done it.'" Disney CEO Bob Igor has put it like this: "The riskiest thing we can do is just maintain the status quo."[23] As for me, I like to say: "If we're doing the same thing over and over again and expecting different results, . . . that's the definition of insanity."[24]

It was a nearly universal belief across the companies in my study that without innovation, an organization is literally standing still. It's not a new insight, but it is one that is becoming more urgent every day. We all need to create space to innovate. Why? Large organizations that don't innovate lose ground to scrappy start-ups with little inertia and bigger ideas. Small organizations that fail to innovate become eclipsed by bigger companies with deeper resources and economies of scale. Innovation today is about survival. That's a given. But I would argue that just as ample a piece of the innovation pie is employee engagement and emotional connectedness.

We explored the connection between innovation, progress, and positivity above. The bottom line is that our best employees want to invent the future. Talented, innovative, creative people from every generation and demographic want to work for innovative companies. They want to be challenged, encouraged to create, and enabled to grow.

In the past, the highest barrier to innovation was organizational structure, with hierarchy and silos acting as bottlenecks. But that's changing. With cross-functional teams, flat organizations, and collaboration becoming the norm, the gap between our desire as individuals to innovate and the ability to execute our ideas is less pronounced. Innovators from all over the organization have a way to float ideas up to the top or spread them across the organization from the edges. The last obstacle is culture. People are In Great Company when organizations set up and sustain a culture that recognizes and rewards innovators and make new ideas everyone's job. It is a massive balancing act to set people free to innovate yet still create real rules and guardrails to keep them focused and on task. But it can be done. These are the best practices from my study, as well as the years of work and insight from the Best Practice Institute.

Stay Future Focused

WD-40 started its life as an innovation. Developed in 1953 to prevent corrosion in nuclear missiles, the breakthrough was named WD-40 because the first 39 attempts to perfect the "water displacement" formula failed. With a single blockbuster product, how does the WD-40 company remain innovative? One big way is to stay future focused.

And it is a very deliberate effort. In 2006, CEO Garry Ridge and his executive team intentionally extended their planning horizon to 10 years out.[25] Until then, business planning was by annum with the occasional attempt to look out three years ahead. As another part of their future focus, they introduced the idea of "unlimited possibilities" into their thinking.

Positive results from this big shift were impressive. For one, cross-functional and cross-regional collaboration have increased dramatically. Employees are trained in strategic thinking, too, and they are invited to offer their input in brainstorming sessions. They have accelerated their global reach too and launched an entire line of WD-40 Specialist products that are currently creating growth in even highly developed markets.

This bigger-picture focus creates an urgency around innovation and gives people permission to think beyond the current moment to what will drive the organization in the future. We may think of innovation mavens like SpaceX (which is ready to send rockets to Mars) as inherently future focused, but this intentional effort to look ahead is equally relevant for companies with traditional products and services. Steelcase, the office furniture innovator, for instance, is famously focused on remaining ahead of the market with patented designs and product updates based on insights they glean by interacting with customers.

Like WD-40, Steelcase has a deliberate focus on balancing future thinking with present concerns. Former longtime CEO Jim Hackett said in the *New York Times* that he used a "bull's-eye" approach: "You put 'now' in the center, and the outer ring is 'near,' and the furthest ring is 'far,'" he said. "What I've argued is that you have to train yourself to work in all three dimensions simultaneously."[26]

The result? Steelcase is the largest furniture manufacture in the world with over 115 years of history to look back on.

Future thinking seems to be working for WD-40 as well. In a recent employee engagement survey, 94.2 percent of employees said, "I am excited about WD-40 Company's future direction," and 99 percent said, "I feel my opinions and values are a good fit with the WD-40 Company culture." And 98.4 percent said, "I love to tell people that I work for WD-40 Company."[27]

Put Risk in Perspective

Creating space for innovation means making room for risk. The most entrepreneurial organizations among us enable experimentation and iteration. In these cases, most attempts at innovation are expected to fail at first—it's baked into the formula. Small bets lead to important lessons that inform future growth.

More and more, large organizations are following their lead. For instance, Intel CEO Brian Krzanich wrote in a memo to employees in 2017: "The new normal for Intel is that we are going to take more risks. The new normal is that we will continue to make bold moves and try new things. We'll make mistakes. Bold doesn't always mean right or perfect. The new normal is that we'll get good at trying new things, determining what works and moving forward."[28]

Organizations like Intel are determined to create innovative cultures that can move quickly to seize opportunities.

Make Innovation for Everyone

Inclusion is a core idea that cuts across all five elements of emotional connectedness. It applies to this aspect of positive future specifically because innovation needs to be a cultural imperative in order to succeed. As we've seen through research, inclusion unlocks innovation by creating an environment where more ideas and different perspectives receive an audience.[29] Luckily, there are myriad ways for companies to give everyone a shot at creating the future.

As one for-instance, Google popularized the idea of side projects, whereby 15 to 20 percent of an employee's time can be spent pursuing relevant ideas and so-called *passion projects*. Although the side project program at Google has been on-again, off-again, it's been wildly productive in generating innovations, with Gmail,

AdSense, and Google Maps all starting out this way.[30] The idea has caught on like wildfire at companies like 3M (their program actually preceded Google's), Intuit, Atlassian, and many others that encourage employees to build unstructured time into their day.

Creating a competition is another way to get people to step forward with the innovation ideas. Stanley Black & Decker has an employee innovation contest where the winner gets the keys to the company Tesla for a month, for instance. Other companies have set up *Shark Tank* style competitions, whereby winners receive funding to pursue a prototype or commercialization of their idea. Yet another brand of innovation contest is the *hackathon*. Generally this is a structured challenge geared to solve a specified problem or build out an idea. Originally a Silicon Valley staple, hackathons have become mainstream in many companies across industries.

From hackathons and side projects to challenges and other contests, there are easy ways for everyone, regardless of job title or level, to come together and try their hand at innovation.

Be Ambidextrous

"Ambidextrous organizations" as described by Charles O'Reilly and Michael Tushman are those that manage to uncover new opportunities even as they work diligently to leverage existing capabilities. More specifically, they "separate their new, exploratory units from their traditional, exploitative ones, allowing for different processes, structures, and cultures; at the same time, they maintain tight links across units at the senior executive level. In other words, they manage organizational separation through a tightly integrated senior team."[31]

This perspective enables companies to pursue innovation on multiple levels simultaneously without pushback or cannibalization. Michael Arena of GM has explained it like this: "Some people need to be fanatically focused on what it takes to design, build, and sell the best possible product or midsize SUV, for instance, and then other people need to be focused on the future game changing ideas like driverless technology, . . . and we create leadership links between the two parts."

This model helps organizations rise above the one-size-fits-all approach to innovation. It also helps them create a positive vision for their future because it keeps enough connections between the levels that each can benefit from what the other learns.

4. Keep Workplace Practices Positive

The last prescription for positive future is extremely straightforward: keep things affirmative. My research shows that many of the most common workplace perks and trappings have scant long-term impact on engagement, but we do know what does play a role—a positive workplace. Research from the University of Michigan and elsewhere shows that positive workplace practices elevate engagement and improve employee effectiveness.[32] In fact, the authors of one study reported, "When organizations institute positive, virtuous practices, they achieve significantly higher levels of organizational effectiveness—including financial performance, customer satisfaction, and productivity. . . . The more the virtuousness, the higher the performance in profitability, productivity, customer satisfaction, and employee engagement."[33]

We see positive practices coming from three places in an organization.

The first source of positivity in the workplace is *organizational culture*. Positive cultures start with commensurate, transparent values and intentional, ongoing follow-through. Companies like Zappos, Warby Parker, and Southwest Airlines are well known for their upbeat, optimistic cultures for a good reason—because they work at it. They design their workplace practices to deliver on that positive vibe, and they hire accordingly. Warby Parker, for one, has a team dedicated to delivering on the positive culture that everyone talks about. Southwest? They have proven that they have a "culture of appreciation" by having never laid off a single employee.[34]

The second source of positivity in the workplace is *leadership*. Yes, the aphorism is true: people don't leave jobs; they leave managers. When a leader is unhappy, negative, or disengaged, it has a cascading effect that disproportionately affects everyone in their sphere of influence. Conversely, leaders who model positive behavior, including optimism, empathy, and enthusiasm, tend to inspire others to act similarly though their good example. It is notable that "emotional contagion" is especially relevant for leaders. When leaders are in a positive mood and behave accordingly, everyone around them follows suit.[35]

The final source of positive workplace practices is *communication*. This is where authentic leadership and culture meet to create trust. Leaders need to speak the truth and do as they say. And employees need to see for themselves that the organizational culture is not only about language but also actions. Communication that rings true in words and deeds delivers on the promise of a positivity future and keeps people connected.

In order to operationalize these ideas, the discussion that follows brings the three sources of positivity together with specific advice for keeping workplace practices positive.

Create a Climate of Optimism

Optimism is the hallmark of a positive workplace. As part of that, employees need to know that they matter, that they are making a positive contribution to the organization, and that their good work has earned them a place at the company now and in the future.

Generally considered to be a worldview, optimism can also be a promise that we build principles and practices around. Coca-Cola, for example, wants to "inspire moments of happiness and optimism." The design firm IDEO, as well, counts optimism as a core value and considers it to be "the engine that allows us to reframe problems and provocations and experiment with new solutions."[36]

Companies can create a climate of optimism by maximizing and developing the strengths of individuals, as opposed to penalizing them for weaknesses. They can remove obstacles that stand in their way by providing resources, encouragement, and coaching. Organizations can also show that they believe in people by empowering them instead of micromanaging. Finally, they can invite more people to solve problems, thereby making them part of the solution and creating a proactive, positive, can-do culture.

Feedforward

Meaningful, targeted feedback is one of the most powerful tools we have to set people up to succeed. And today we have many more ways to offer and receive feedback. Pulse surveys, mobile apps, and new tools for 360-degree reviews all make it possible use instant insights to improve our performance. But there's a catch. Oftentimes feedback has a negative impact on future performance. Delivered in the wrong way, feedback triggers a fear response and puts us on the defensive. Even worse, focusing on past events that are impossible to change makes us feel helpless and reinforces negative behaviors.

Luckily, there is a far better way. I have found that people are In Great Company when they view feedback as feed*forward*. Coined by Marshall Goldsmith, author of *What Got You Here Won't Get You There*, feedforward fits the positive future paradigm perfectly because it focuses on what we can do better. It uses an appreciative approach to provide information on future actions. These are the behavioral changes that underlie the principle of feedforward:

▶ Focus on maximizing and developing strengths in the future, instead of cataloging past weaknesses.

▶ Use what you know about "what went wrong in the past" to describe "how to be great in the future."

▶ Don't rank people with numbers or categorize or label them as good or bad based on past behavior.

▶ Elevate people with coaching. Don't lecture to them.

▶ Be specific, and focus on meaningful future behavior. Don't provide a meaningless information dump.

▶ Include multiple data points over time—not feedback from a single manager.

▶ Use the feedforward approach as part of everyday management. Don't save advice for an annual discussion that is tied to compensation.

▶ Above all, instead of providing negative or positive feedback, focus on providing future-oriented options and solutions.

Feedforward is the killer app not only for delivering feedback that will be received positively, but also for creating emotional connectedness. Taking a coaching approach to performance management and demonstrating that you genuinely want employees to succeed in the future brings people closer together every time.

Start with Yes, And

"*Yes, and*" are powerfully positive words. Saying "yes, and" to a business idea, a request for coaching, a bid for more responsibility, or even just an offer to get coffee together is affirming, active, and empowering for both parties. Saying "and" after "yes" gives you the opportunity to address your requests and needs to your "yes." In contrast, starting with the word *no* or other negative language, such as the word *but*, shuts the other person down, negates the other person's requests or feelings, eats away at trust, and stops action in its tracks. We can't always say a firm yes, but using positivity as our default creates a way to step away from our comfort zone, think differently, and consider the possibilities.

Probably the person who has the most notable predisposition to positivity in business today is Mr. Optimism himself, Jeff Bezos. In order to encourage Amazon's managers to give the green light to more ideas and experiments, Bezos put into practice what he calls "the institutional yes." That is, he challenges leaders to default to the positive rather than shutting down new thinking.

Bezos has other positive policies that get people to say yes. One is called "working backward," whereby product developers write the press release for an innovation before it's even developed—to help them start with the customer and show what success looks like before seeking approval to proceed.

Saying yes is just one example of positive language. The idea is to choose to speak in a way that creates a positive environment, fosters innovation, and enables forward momentum.

Whether by leveraging passion, managing change, creating space to innovate, or simply creating a positive workplace, giving people the gift of a positive future not only keeps people connected in a positive way but also sustains that connection and sets people up to be In Great Company.

POSITIVE FUTURE: EXECUTIVE SUMMARY

Positive Best Practices	Ground Rules
Leverage passion.	Let purpose drive passion. Turn passion into products. Let passion pivot. Look for passionate persuaders. Put passion in its place.
Turn change into a positive.	Neutralize the pain of change. Get positive with "deviants." Offer more ways to change.
Create space to innovate.	Stay future focused. Put risk in perspective. Make innovation for everyone. Be ambidextrous.
Keep workplace practices positive.	Create a climate of optimism. Feedforward. Start with *yes, and*.

CHAPTER 5

ALIGNMENT OF VALUES

When the popular outdoor clothing company Patagonia printed an advertisement on Black Friday in 2011, they were one among many. Hundreds of retailers from Target and Best Buy to Home Depot had all promised extended store hours and one-day sales. What set Patagonia apart by a country mile was their ad telling customers in bold lettering: "Don't Buy This Jacket."

The full-page notice in the *New York Times* contained a large photo of a popular Patagonia jacket, urging consumers to put down their credit cards and consider resisting "the culture of consumption." It was a maverick move for Patagonia, and it was right on the mark—and on the money. The company's counterintuitive strategy led to a surprising surge in positive publicity and delivered record-breaking seasonal sales.[1] The antimaterialism message and other similar brand-appropriate moves by Patagonia elevated the organization to cult status not only among customers but also among employees. And the gesture was authentic. It was a proof point that reinforced their stance on social issues such as protecting the planet, and it fully aligned with their established corporate values.

Alignment of values is often viewed as subjective and intangible, which makes it even more important to agree on a concrete definition. In my work, I view it as the condition whereby an organization's core beliefs or values are wholly embraced and implemented by employees and leaders. *Alignment of values informs a company's culture, exemplifies their reason for being, drives decision-making, and establishes a common framework for how the organization and its employees can grow together and move forward into the future.* What's more, values alignment emerged in our study as a basic requirement for creating a workplace where employees feel like they are In Great Company.

Patagonia is a *paragon* when it comes to values alignment. Take their mission statement: "Build the best product, cause no unnecessary harm, use business to inspire and implement solutions to the environmental crisis."[2] This tells us that Patagonia not only takes customer needs and environmental sustainability seriously but also considers each to be a reinforcing mechanism for the other. In pushing back on Black Friday buying, the organization was simultaneously looking out for its consumers as well as their shared beliefs around conspicuous consumption—and publicly living into its mission.

The result? Today sales continue to surge, brand recognition is high, and employee turnover is "freakishly low."[3] Values alignment creates an undeniable connection among employees. In fact, Patagonia's past HR director told *Workforce* magazine that the company represents the culture of its employees as much as the employees are the custodians of it.[4] That's emotional connectedness in action. When people buy into a common belief system within their company, and the bond proves to be sustained and authentic, it establishes genuine trust, and employees are able to find more meaning in their work.

Alignment of values is a potent state of being that keeps people connected and encourages them to perform at their best. Howard Behar, founding president of Starbucks, told me about the time early in Starbucks's history, when he and Howard Schultz witnessed the power of values alignment:

> As 7,000 or more of us streamed into the Key Arena in Seattle for our first ever "all-hands-on" meeting of store managers, Howard Schultz and I sat and watched in wonder. Their energy and camaraderie was tremendous. Almost simultaneously, we said to each other "How the heck did this happen? How did we get here?" The answer was simple. The people made it happen. They believed in a greater purpose, which they helped create. We created it together, and that's what made Starbucks successful.[5]

Alignment of values is part of what makes Starbucks successful—and the same can be said for every other great company that endures over time. They cocreate core values that resonate with employees, and emotionally competent leaders actively embody these values, building them into the core of the business and creating the In Great Company dynamic. Memorable, meaningful values that employees believe in are the heartbeat of every great company, and without them there is no foundational identity upon which to thrive and grow.

Why Values Align Us

Jim Collins and Jerry Porras made the case in *Built to Last* that visionary companies live by a set of inherent core values that engage employees and create a sense of shared purpose beyond making money.[6] Later, author Patrick Lencioni put a complementary stake in the ground, saying that core values "are the source of a company's distinctiveness" and "need to be integrated into every employee-related process" from hiring to firing.[7]

Ample additional research, including my own, corroborates their findings: value alignment is a core component of organizational success. I will get to the "how to align values" below; for now, let's look at why. Why did values alignment land in the top five as an element of EC that puts people In Great Company? Three reasons.

First, meaning really matters to people, and it keeps them connected to each other and the organization. Study after study shows that people want to join together to invest their time, effort, and intellect in something that is bigger than themselves.[8] *My own research shows that greater employee engagement and increased productivity are not based on bigger paychecks, off-site retreats, Ping-Pong tables, free lunches, or even additional paid leave. It's deeper and more intrinsic ideals like alignment of values.* Glassdoor reported similar findings. Based on a survey of 615,000 Glassdoor users, "the top predictor of workplace satisfaction is not pay. It is the culture and values of the organization."[9]

Oftentimes, we connect the search for meaning at work with millennials. They move faster from company to company, embrace gig economy dynamics, and reportedly work for "purpose over paycheck." But the truth is that the shared-values imperative is much larger than any single generation. According to research, 68 percent of us do not think businesses do enough to instill a sense of meaningful purpose in our work culture.[10]

The bottom line is that all of us want to work for organizations we admire and respect and those that stand for the things that we believe in. Values run deep, and aligning them means more to us than almost anything else.

Next, values alignment guides ethical decision-making. One of the first and easily the best-known example of a corporate credo or values-based mission statement is Johnson & Johnson's. Created by former chairman Robert Wood Johnson in 1943, just before the company went public, the credo spells out the company's responsibility to its customers, employees, communities, and shareholders. According to J&J's website, the credo contains "the values that guide our decision-making" in a way that "challenges us to put the needs and well-being of the people we serve first."[11]

These promises could be seen as elegant but empty if J&J failed to live by those promises. But consider, for example, the decisive action taken by the company in 1982, in what proved to be their most public crisis to date—seven deaths over a period of several weeks in metropolitan Chicago as a result of criminal drug tampering and cyanide-laced capsules of Extra-Strength Tylenol. At the time, the Tylenol brand accounted for 17 percent of the company's net income, and it was the drug maker's bestselling product. Not only their reputation but also their business—not to mention the lives of their customers—hung in the balance during this dramatic time.

True to its credo, J&J's put consumers first in a way that no other company had before. Instead of delaying action or shifting blame, Chairman James Burke immediately and voluntarily pulled 31 million bottles of Tylenol from store shelves and spent $100 million on the initial recall and relaunch of Tylenol capsules in new tamperproof packaging. The fast and transparent handling of the tragic incident not only made it clear that the company made its most important decisions with its values credo in mind, but it also prompted a revolution in product safety standards. After that, tamperproof seals and enhanced security controls during manufacturing became the industry standard.[12]

Burke was able to make difficult decisions quickly under incredible pressure because J&J's values made it very clear what actions were required.

Finally, values alignment matters because values themselves tap into what make us human: how we connect to each other. With social media and ever-present connectivity breaking down the walls between our personal and professional lives, it becomes less feasible to compartmentalize our belief systems and keep our values under wraps at work. If our organization acts unethically, it becomes a reflection on us. But if it goes the extra mile to honor customers, we instantly feel the halo effect.

This—the human factor—brings together all three reasons values alignment ranks high as an element of being In Great Company. With artificial intelligence and machine learning trending as sources of future business and innovation, values like honesty, empathy, love, respect, and creativity mean more to people than ever, and organizations do well when they enshrine them as part of the values that they call their own. Whether for decision-making, crisis management, or creating meaning, values connect us to each other because they cut straight to the core of what makes us human.

Why Values Alignment Is Elusive

Like many things, creating corporate values and building a workforce that is equipped to adopt and exhibit common core beliefs is easier said than done. In fact, based on all that I see every day in my work with organizations, companies seem to fall short at this tough task. And the research concurs. According to Gallup, only 27 percent of employees believe in their company values. The same study found that there is commonly a gap between a company's desired culture and the culture employees actually experience.[13] The effect is inconsistent decision-making and a disengaged workforce.

Why is it so difficult to achieve the ideal I have been describing?

One culprit is the fast pace of change. Unlike when Johnson & Johnson was established, today companies can be founded fast with a particular business objective, only to evolve quickly and become something altogether different. Changing to respond to opportunities as they arise is part of the start-up ethos. (Twitter started as a hub for podcasts before it became the master of microblogging, and Flickr was an online role-playing game before its founders made the shift to photo sharing.) Pivots are a means of survival for early-stage ventures, but these shifts in mission can make it more difficult to remain consistent and live by one set of core values.

One could easily suggest that alignment of values is not a realistic or appropriate expectation for fast-growth companies. Yet, I would argue that creating consistency around core beliefs is necessary for every organization, regardless of the logistical challenges brought on by change. After all, while Silicon Valley is famous for business model innovation and venture capital, it is also notorious for the type of cultural transgressions that nearly brought down Uber in 2017.

Similar to fast change, a second barrier to values alignment is short-term thinking. *When organizations and executives bow to unrealistic pressure to perform, making decisions based purely on current quarterly earnings over sustainable objectives, enduring values are often brushed aside or forgotten.* Enron is the textbook case. Although one of its corporate values was "Integrity: We work with customers and prospects openly, honestly, and sincerely," the firm was nonetheless felled following a massive accounting scandal that sent executives to prison and caused the dissolution of its public accounting firm, Arthur Andersen.

The last major barrier to values alignment is a lack of executive sponsorship and support. Low bandwidth leads well-intentioned leaders and midlevel managers to give short shift to this important driver of emotional connectedness. Many organizations take the time to craft values statements, but they fail to do the more difficult job of creating a culture that respects and lives by the ideals they set forth. This barrier becomes higher as organizations grow and values become diluted by size and scale and accountability breaks down. The consequence? When an organization touts a set of core values and then fails it live into them, the fallout is amplified.

Take Wells Fargo, for example, whose original mission statement included the promise to do what's right for customers.[14] But that idea was publicly called into question when a whistleblower forced the organization to admit that thousands of Wells Fargo employees had charged millions of customers fraudulent fees for bank accounts those customers had not authorized in order to meet unrealistic sales goals set forth by management. And if the actions themselves were not damaging enough, the fallout was amplified because the offense went against the organization's publicly stated core values.

As a milestone of being In Great Company, an organization's core values can serve to make work more meaningful for employees, but only if they are aligned across the organization and everyone works together with them in mind.

Alignment of Values: The Best Practices Playbook

Is there a secret sauce for values alignment? Zappos thinks so. The Las Vegas–based e-tailer is so confident about its ability to create a positive culture where core values cascade across the organization that the company built a business around teaching it to others. As part of that, companies from around the world attend a three-day boot camp about how Zappos's 1,400 employees "live their 10 WOW values." And why not? Zappos is a role model for how to infuse culture and unify an organization using core values.

And there are other role models as well, spanning the spectrum of industries and types. Some are start-ups, and others are a few of the largest and most established companies in the world. In exploring the steps below, I will mention Zappos as well as some of the companies I've coached as they built a competency for values alignment. Above all, my intent here is to distill the basic building blocks, based on my research, so that any organization can create, sustain, and scale values alignment as part of the In Great Company ethos of success (Figure 5.1).

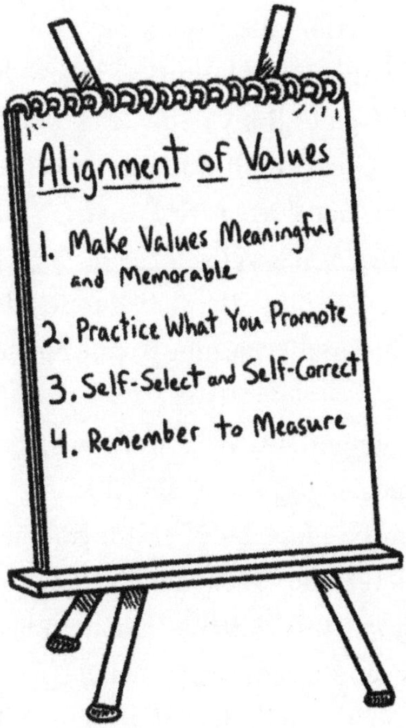

FIGURE 5.1

1. Make Values Meaningful and Memorable

A main reason many of the companies I work with can't earn a high score on the Emotional Connectedness Index (ECI) for values alignment is pretty simple: they don't have explicit core values. At least not ones that resonate with employees and guide the organization in a way that enables them to be their best. Many wonder:

"Do we even need to put a stake in the ground with a formal values statement? It is worth our time and effort with so many other pressing issues competing for our attention? Is this really important?"

It is if you want to be In Great Company.

Howard Behar put it this way: "At the beginning, I thought, 'Well, it's just a statement. How big could that be?' But it was everything. . . . It's been the glue that's held us together and the driving force that defines who we are. . . . It was that way when we were starting out, and it hasn't changed one bit."

Behar is talking about Starbucks's core values. Johnson & Johnson has The Credo. Jim Collins talks about a BHAG: "Big Hairy Audacious Goal." Innovation guru Salim Ismail refers to a MTP: "Massive Transformative Purpose." Mission; purpose; values; raison d'être. Whatever you call it, I'm referring to an organization's core aspiration. The shared rationale that gets every employee out of bed in the morning to collaborate with colleagues for another day.

The title is unimportant. What really matters is that your core values are both meaningful and memorable.

They need to be meaningful and memorable because they have a massive job to do. They guide people to act and inspire them to perform in a way that binds them to others in service of a higher purpose (above and beyond making money for the company). Whole Foods's core values statement is deeply meaningful and memorable because of the words they chose: "With great courage, integrity, and love—we embrace our responsibility to co-create a world where each of us, our communities, and our planet can flourish. All the while, celebrating the sheer love and joy of food."[15] Not many corporate values contain the word "love," not once but twice, and those that do send a message to employees about how they should feel about their work.

Values statements that are meaningful and memorable demonstrate to employees and customers that the organization stands for more than any one product or service. Patagonia, for instance, has a mission statement that is more about preserving the environment than selling outdoor apparel. That sends a strong message to people who like to climb, hike, or surf: we stand for the same things that you do.

Last, values statements that are meaningful and memorable align everyone in the organization around specific ideals. Johnson & Johnson's credo says that the company is responsible first to its customers, then to its employees, the community, and the stockholders—in that order.[16] That's pretty specific. Core values need to unequivocally define what the organization stands for, and they need to aggressively inspire employees to not only comply to but also to come up with creative solutions, together with colleagues, that live into the ideals.

In reality, creating core values that are meaningful and memorable is more about having the right mindset than following one perfect process. It starts with openness and honest self-reflection, and eventually it may look something like an iterative brainstorming session. For some, meaningful, memorable core values are dreamed up on day one by a few visionary founders, but more likely they emerge with help from people working across the organization at every level who can keep the following prescriptive principles in mind.

Get Existential

In order to engage the organization and bring people together, core values need to answer big-picture questions that cut to the heart of the matter: "Why are we here?" "What makes us special?" "Why should we [employees, customers, stakeholders] bother?" These and other fundamental questions connect back to a company's larger purpose and help us create values that are magnanimous and motivating.

Be Aspirational

Core values can and should help leaders get a fix on the organization as they want it to be in the future, as opposed to describing exactly what it is right now. In other words, core values are as much a turnaround tool as they are a guide for decision-making in the present. When Steve Jobs rejoined Apple in 1997, the "Think Different" slogan was more than a marketing campaign, it was an aspirational phrase to challenge employees and remind them what Apple at its best was all about.

Aspirational core values bring people together and actively mobilize them. And the ideas themselves should do most of the hard work, but the words themselves, as well, should be engaging, relatable, and active. Zappos's first value, "Deliver WOW Through Service," like their other nine values, is active, jargon free, and designed to excite.

As part of that broader aspiration, meaningful core values don't focus on any particular product or service. Touchstones that act as glue to hold the organization together are far less business specific, and instead they are timeless and inspirational. The vision at IKEA, for instance, is "To create a better everyday life for the many people."

Cocreate Core Values

Starbucks's employees helped create their core values. Likewise, Zappos founder Tony Hsieh included the entire company in the process. Why include more people in core values creation? So many reasons. Employees must embody core values (that's values alignment) in order to help make any company truly great. With that, they are closest to customers and have the clearest ideas about what the market wants. Diverse perspectives yield greater creativity. And so on. The bottom line is that core values need to be shared by all employees, so everyone should take part in their creation is some way.

Think Broadly About Audience

Not all companies need core values with words like *WOW* or *love*. As active and aspirational as they need to be, they should also be appropriate and speak to employees and customers in a language that they can immediately understand. The Build-A-Bear company has six simple core values including "Di-bear-sity" and "Colla-bear-ate." It doesn't get much more culture specific than that.

Core values should speak to multiple stakeholders. Johnson & Johnson, Warby Parker, and Wegmans, among many others, mention employees specifically in their core values. This puts their commitment to people on record, and it serves to acknowledge the pay-it-forward principal: companies with a strong reputation as "best workplaces" are often exceptional at serving customers.

2. Practice What You Promote

Creating meaningful core values that permeate corporate cultures sets an organization up for sustainable success. That sounds like an easy win, but there's a very big *if* inherent in this. *Companies with clear core values are on the path to being In Great Company if they are insistent and consistent in how they exhibit their values in everything from daily decisions to strategy setting.* Hollow core values create a demoralized workforce, while authentic, fully integrated values create emotional connectedness. It's that simple.

John Tu, CEO and cofounder of Kingston Technologies, the world's largest independent manufacturer of flash memory products, told me that actively practicing the values you promote is about the small details as much as the big decisions. "Doing what you say you will at work and showing employees that you care," he said, creates a bond between people and mobilizes them "to love coming to work every day."[17] It is all about being active and authentic. Kingston's core values include "loyalty" and "investing in our employees," among others.

"You can put anything you want into writing and paint it on your conference room wall for people to look at," he told me. "But that's just propaganda. What's important to us? Doing it. People need to witness core values in action."

Tu, a first-generation Chinese immigrant who believes deeply in the American dream and sharing his "luck and good fortune" with Kingston employees, walked the talk in a dramatic way in 1996 when he and his partner, David Sun, sold 80 percent of Kingston to the Japanese firm Softbank Corp. As part of that, they set aside $100 million in profits from the sale and awarded unprecedented bonuses to their American employees. In many cases, the bonuses ranged from $100,000 to $300,000.[18]

Tu and Sun later bought the company back, and today the $6.5 billion business employs more than 3,000 people and has earned a place on *Fortune*'s "Best Companies to Work for in America" list in large part by authentically embodying their core values.

Tu understands that it is impossible to achieve values alignment unless the organization walks the talk from the C suite down to the shop floor. Executive leaders set the tone, make the strategic decisions, and create a foundation for the corporate culture. Middle managers interact with employees and engage in performance management and planning. Employees and associates are often closest in proximity to customers and shape products and services accordingly. All of these activities, relationships, and interactions are ongoing opportunities to embody the company's core ideals and exhibit values alignment in ways, like those that follow, that put your organization In Great Company.

Overcommunicate Your Values

When asked, 54 percent of employees say their company's purpose is not clearly conveyed.[19] Although it's critical to get beyond talking to actually living them, employees should understand the core values and where they fit within the context of the company. Yet, none of us likes to sit through obligatory formal training sessions.

Companies need to get creative, then, and experiment with better ways to explore shared values. Some organizations do this through informal coaching, while others try hands-on opportunities such as encouraging people to volunteer in the community with their colleagues during work hours. Life is Good, the Boston-based apparel company has effectively built their business around their primary core value: optimism. Not only are they known by employees to be a "glass half-full" company, but they also plaster optimistic drawings and saying across their popular T-shirts and baseball hats, and customers line up to buy them to be a part of the famously upbeat experience.

Regardless of the program or process, the end result should be a clear understanding of the shape values take in the organization and the ways that people live them every day.

Live by the Values You Promote

The degree to which people believe their company lives the values it promotes is effectively proportionate to employee engagement and satisfaction.[20] While there is no single best way for an organization and its leaders and employees to walk the talk, everyday behavior as well as big-picture decisions should distinctly reflect core values.

Patagonia's decision to print its "Don't Buy This Jacket" ad was a clear value play, but so is its ongoing custom of encouraging employees to leave work during the day to surf or fish. Both moves embody the organization's environmentalist vibe in support of minimalism and an appreciation of sustainable living and outdoor activities.

Act with Empathy and Compassion

Values mean something to people because they tap into our deep desire for higher-order ideas such as connection, compassion, and empathy. Acting on these deeper ideas and including them in your core values strengthen the connection between employees and the organization.

Jeanette K. Winters, SVP and chief human resources officer at Igloo Products, told me about the efforts the organization took following Hurricane Harvey and its devastating effects on communities in the Houston area. Located in Katy, Texas, 30 miles due west from downtown Houston, several communities in Katy itself were left under water, and many areas were forced to evacuate. According to Winters, the families of 53 Igloo employees were very significantly affected by the hurricane, and 15 lost everything including their homes and cars. Igloo's response? They not only spent a quarter of a million dollars to pay people for a week who could not come into work, but they also made food and supplies available and gave out 23,000 coolers to their associates and to local families that didn't have electricity.[21]

"These efforts to support families brought all of us closer together," Winters said. "Leadership set the tone, and we answered that call to help each other. More than anything, I think it said something powerful to people about our values and the vision of the leaders here."

Lead by Example

One common thread that cut across much of my research for *In Great Company* is this: leaders need to do what they say. Because core values are such a primary component of company culture, the example set by leaders—how they communicate and publicly embody values—may be the single most important element for creating trust and setting the company up for values alignment.

3. Self-Select and Self-Correct

Ever wonder why someone can be extremely successful in one organization, only to underperform in another, or vice versa? That is values alignment. *You can train people for skills development and coach them to deepen their relationships . . . but values? They come from within.* The best moments to consider values alignment and culture is during the hiring process. In my work with organizations, I've been a part of three hiring phases that are prime opportunities to actively influence values fit.

The first is the *recruiting phase*. This is the initial opportunity for candidates to opt in or out based on their core values. It works best when companies lead with values in the marketplace and are crystal clear with recruiters in all written material designed to attract talent. This degree of transparency is far easier when an organization's brand is well known for its culture. For instance, individuals who don't want a culture based on meritocracy are unlikely to step forward for a job at GE, where meritocracy and commitment to personal excellence are clearly stated core values. Likewise, one look at Netflix recruiting materials and you'd know that they "keep only our highly effective people" and "focus on results over process." That type of specificity and transparency allows people to self-select a culture that suits their needs and skip those that don't resonate with their values.

Next is the *interviewing phase*. This is when organizations get their first pass at assessing value fit. While many companies skew their interview process toward experience and skills over mind-set and values, the calculus is shifting. Zappos, for one, skips the generic approach by crafting interview questions that screen for each of their core values. In *Harvard Business Review*, Zappos CEO Tony Hsieh said, "Be Humble is probably the core value that ends up affecting our hiring decisions the most." He went on to say that they interview scores of experienced, smart, and talented people, but they always take a pass if the individual lacks humility. Hsieh said it's all part of "protecting the company culture and sticking to our core values."[22]

Finally, there's the *onboarding phase*. Onboarding is your first and best opportunity to formally teach and train employees about core values. If the recruiting process worked well, new hires will already be privy to these priorities. Still, at some organizations, onboarding presentations are the only time when a C-suite hire will be reading from the same slide deck as a summer intern—because the same core values apply to everyone.

And onboarding doesn't end after day one. At Jazz Pharmaceuticals, where core values are stated prominently in every offer letter, six-month anniversaries are a strategic inflection point and an opportunity to measure the success of every new hire. The metrics? Eric Fink, Jazz CHRO, told me, "First, we look at the Net Promotor Score—are they happy in their job and would they refer the company to a friend? Second, how are they performing against their objectives and specifically against values?" Fink told me that focusing on values from the beginning is important because "the success and happiness of our people are what makes us great."[23]

Putting values at the center of the hiring process requires resolve. As one founding CEO told me, "We hire for ideal fit. That means we hire slow for culture, and we fire fast for the same reason." The following are some of the ways to capture that ideal fit and focus on creating values alignment to be In Great Company.

Prepare Candidates to Self-Select

Give candidates clear guidance on corporate values to help them decide for themselves if it's a good fit. Fink says that Jazz created a detailed values blueprint for recruits and new hires. "You have a choice about whom you're employed with," he said. "At Jazz, performance isn't just about getting stuff done. It's also about how you live our values each and every day. It's important that people can relate to that."

Screen for Values

People's values preferences are not listed on their résumés. And often, it's only top executives who undergo rigorous qualitative assessments and behavioral screening to isolate values strengths and offer a formal prediction about fit. But there are other ways to screen for values. For instance, inexpensive HR software can be customized to help assess candidates' thinking and compatibility on core values. Similarly, algorithms are used more and more to screen candidates based on values and their chances for success.

In addition, observing how candidates interact with each other can offer yet another valuable data point on fit. Alan Lewis, founder and chairman at Grand Circle Corporation, said, "Our process includes a group interview, in which multiple candidates interview for various open jobs at the same time. We observe candidates undertaking unique, and often quirky, challenges and interacting with each other. Candidates act out scenarios that show us whether or not they exhibit our core values—open and courageous communication, risk taking, speed, quality, teamwork, and thriving in change."[24]

Ask About Specific Situations

One way to determine values fit is to ask candidates to tell a story or describe a specific situation in their past jobs that illustrates an affinity for the values you are promoting. This encourages them to dig deep and provide meaningful specifics. Another way is to present a situation in which relevant values come into play and ask how they would react. This tests their leadership instincts and shows how they might act under pressure. Regardless of the format, try to approach the values question from several different angles to see if a candidate has a consistent, authentic perspective.

Consider the Level or Function of an Employee

Although everyone needs to align around the same values, it is important to take job level or function into account to understand where values intersect with an individual's everyday work. For instance, executives must be able lead with values in mind, whereas line workers interact with customers and make everyday decisions based on their understanding of how to apply the corporate values. In other words, alignment of values is critical at all levels, although perhaps for different reasons.

4. Remember to Measure

People know they are In Great Company when every employee is set up to contribute fully, regardless of job title, and they hold themselves and others accountable for results and objectives. When it comes to the numbers and other quantitative objectives, accountability has become seamless over the years with state-of-the-art sales tracking and performance management systems. But measuring values alignment is something altogether different and more difficult. Qualitative expectations are subjective, anecdotal, and traditionally relegated to the tail end of performance conversations.

But more recently, with corporate culture understood to be a key driver of competitive advantage, greater attention and insistence has been dedicated to managing and tracking core values alignment. Tom Kolditz, retired brigadier general and head of behavioral science and leadership at West Point, said that the U.S. military is a longtime standard bearer for enforcing values alignment.

"One of the fundamental roles of any leader preparing for combat, or anywhere in the military, is to enforce the value structure of the organization," he said. "And when it comes to values, whether it is mutual respect, loyalty, or integrity, . . . we can never settle."[25]

Speaking about values in all organizations, not the military exclusively, Kolditz (currently executive director of the Doerr Institute for New Leaders at Rice University) went on to say, "You can negotiate on other things, but institutional values are not fungible."

His perspective is becoming ever more prevalent, as values-first companies like Netflix and Southwest Airlines reinforce and measure values alignment as part of 360-degree performance reviews, compensation conversations, promotion decisions, and exit interviews. Likewise, Novozymes, a Copenhagen-based biotechnology firm producing industrial enzymes used globally in everything from detergents and beer to fuel, has embedded measurement of its core value—sustainability—into nearly everything it does.

Founded as a spinoff from the pharmaceutical company Novo Nordisk in 2000, Novozymes has positioned sustainability as the most visible offering in its value proposition, with three stated areas of strategic focus:

1. Making the world aware of the sustainability benefits of biotechnology,
2. Creating new business from sustainability, and

3. Building sustainability capabilities across the
organization to enable all employees to contribute.[26]

As part of that, Novozymes's leaders have developed a wide
range of performance targets, with corresponding bonus and stock
option programs for employees and management. According to
Claus Stig Pedersen, head of corporate sustainability at Novozymes,
one notable result of this effort at measurement was succeeding in
decoupling growth in sales and profits from growth in energy, water
consumption, and CO_2 emissions. In other words, measuring for
core values gave them multiple ways to measure success.

Pedersen said their values-centric approach has enhanced their
reputation among customers, partners, and even competitors.
Even more, "the pride Novozymes's employees feel from contrib-
uting to making a more sustainable world" is seen by executives as
a major business benefit.

In a business environment where companies compete to recruit and retain top talent, achieving values alignment through
performance measurement tools, such as those that follow, can
be invaluable for creating the emotional connectedness that keeps
people engaged and performing their best.

Keep Top Management Accountable

Developing performance measurement systems that succeed from
both a business and values perspective requires buy-in and ownership from top managers. For instance, Novozymes has a cross-
functional corporate sustainability board. The board, chaired by
Pedersen, has eight members, all senior leaders who head the company's key functions, including business development, finance,
production, marketing, and procurement. When senior leaders
develop the company's sustainability targets and programs, are responsible for implementing them, and are held accountable for

their success, business and sustainability become linked from the top down.

Create the Business Case

How do you get executives who are driven by production and profit targets to tie performance measures to values? By making the business case. Whole Foods co-CEO John Mackey, for example, frequently articulates the business case for the organization's values-driven business in his blog posts and interviews, as he did in this letter to stakeholders, where he wrote the following:

> We walk our talk when it comes to our core values. Our primary goal is to satisfy and delight our customers. Through constant experimentation and innovation, we are redefining the retail food marketplace and further differentiating our shopping experience from other food retailers. We continue to expand and adapt our product offering in ways that speak to our core customers and to our authenticity and leadership role within natural and organic products. . . . Our business model is very successful and continues to benefit all of our stakeholders. We are executing at a high level, continuing to produce higher sales growth, comparable store sales increases and sales per square foot than our public competitors.[27]

Understanding the impact values have on business makes it more feasible for everyone in the organization to find ways to factor them into performance management systems.

Remember to Track the How

A long-term perspective and a strategy that delivers sustained success requires going beyond quarterly earnings data. Leaders need to measure not only what was accomplished by people in any given time period but also how it was achieved. Author and hospitality entrepreneur Chip Conley put it this way: "You look at manager say, 'Hey, great P&L' or 'Great cash flow statement,' but if the way they got that was to fire half their staff, piss off customers, or charge them so much, that's not a sustainable business strategy. Generally speaking, sometimes being able to measure relationships with customers, employees, or vendors is a better way to get a sense of the long-term sustainability of the effectiveness of a manager or leader."[28]

Jazz Pharmaceuticals, as well, redesigned its performance management system to include values alignment: "We want to be really transparent about this because, for us, what you achieve and how you achieve it are both equally important," Fink told me.

Measuring and managing for core values—including how things are accomplished—allows organizations to go deeper than numbers and collect many different types of data.

Use Partners to Keep You Accountable

Organizations that make customers and vendors a part of their values agenda are more likely to hold themselves accountable for delivering on their promises. Novozymes abides by this philosophy, which serves to underscore the company's belief that achieving sustainable development requires collaboration between the public and private sectors. As part of their "Sustainable Energy for All" initiative, Novozymes's customers reduced their CO_2 emissions by a combined total of 60 million tons in 2014. Pedersen said that is equal to taking 25 million cars off the roads.

Sharing something as significant as values puts people In Great Company every time. The excellent benefit of values alignment, even beyond the EC it creates among colleagues and the company, is that it extends naturally to customers and other stakeholders in a way that drives performance and keeps everyone aligned.

ALIGNMENT OF VALUES: EXECUTIVE SUMMARY

Positive Best Practices	Ground Rules
Make values meaningful and memorable.	Get existential. Be aspirational. Cocreate core values. Think broadly about audience.
Practice what you promote.	Overcommunicate your values. Live by the values you promote. Act with empathy and compassion. Lead by example.
Self-select and self-correct.	Prepare candidates to self-select. Screen for values. Ask about specific situations. Consider the level or function of an employee.
Remember to measure.	Keep top management accountable. Create the business case. Remember to track the how. Use partners to keep you accountable.

CHAPTER 6

RESPECT

Howard Behar shared his recollection of what I consider to be the iconic story of mutual respect and the example set by Howard Schultz at Starbucks. The story itself dates back to their early days of the company, and I want to tell it in Howard Behar's own words to keep it in context and provide the full effect:

> It was 1989, and I was the new VP of operations at Starbucks, and Howard [Schultz] was the 34-years-old CEO. One day I heard from a store manager—a young guy named Jim who had been with Starbucks nearly from the beginning. He called me to say, "I'd like to meet with you and Howard [Schultz]."
>
> "Sure," I said. "But maybe there's something I can do for you, Jim. What is it?" Jim responded: "No, I really need to talk to both of you."
>
> I said, "Okay," and promised to set up the meeting.
>
> The day arrived and Jim came to the front desk. I got him, and we sat on the little loveseat in Howard's office, and we made small talk while Howard finished up a phone call. Howard hung up, and he and

Jim started talking, because they'd known each other for a while. Eventually I did what all A-type personalities do. I said, "So, Jim, what can we do for you?"

Jim just looked at us both and said, "Well, I want to tell you that I'm dying. I'm dying of AIDS."

This was in the early days of the epidemic, and we didn't know a lot about AIDS. Was it a virus that was catching? What was it? A tear came down Howard's face, and I sat there, kind of in shock. I had no idea how Howard would respond.

Howard said, "Well, Jim, what can we do for you?"

Jim told us: "I'd like to work as long as I can, and I don't know how long that will be."

Howard just looked at him, and he said, "Jim, you can work until you don't want to work anymore."

Then Howard asked him a question: "How are you going to support yourself when you can't work anymore?"

Jim said, "There's lot of agencies now that are starting to give help to people that are dying of AIDS, and there's hospice and all sorts of things." Howard just looked at him and said, "Absolutely not, Jim. You will be on our payroll until you die, until you pass away. We will continue to pay you as if you were working here."

Howard asked him a second question. He said, "Who's going to pay for your healthcare?"

Jim had the same answer, "There's people that are helping."

Howard said immediately, "No, you'll be on our healthcare system."[1]

It's a pretty amazing story. Now, let me put it into even clearer focus. Starbucks was losing money at the time. They had no idea they would become the iconic business they soon grew to be. Here's Howard, a young CEO in the food service industry, not really knowing whether AIDS was a contagious disease. You can work until you don't want to work anymore. And not only that, you'll be on our healthcare.

Not only could an "average" employee make just one phone call and get in for a meeting with the CEO—which is notable in and of itself—but then to have the CEO step up and react with such empathy for his situation. What kind of message do you think that sent in the early days of the company about respect and the values of the organization?

According to Behar, who was an enormously influential figure at Starbucks, serving as president and later as a director of the company, "I realized right then that I was in the right place because I knew that I could do anything for anybody who was in need. That's the message the encounter sent out to the whole organization."

There were a lot of things that made Starbucks successful. They were brilliant about market segmentation—setting up shops in vibrant communities and catering to discerning coffee clientele. They turned the business into a consumer experience worth paying for with friendly baristas and a warm, ambient environment. Their progressive stance on social issues, as well, appealed to customers. But above all, of course, it was the culture. It was the way leaders treated employees, how employees treated each other, and how they treated customers—with respect. Jim was able to go right to Howard Schultz to tell him the news, and Howard stepped up without any hesitation.

Behar summed it up, "When you have that respect at the core of the company, then that's how you treat the people we call customers. But it all started with how we treated each other. We were ferocious about treating people with respect. That's exactly what drove the company."

Why Respect Connects Us

Of the five main elements of emotional connectedness that make up the In Great Company approach, respect in many ways is the linchpin that connects all the rest. (See the box "Why Respect Is the EC Spark.") In fact, the respondents in my study reported that they are far more willing to put in extra effort (four times more likely) when they feel genuine respect in the workplace. My follow-up interviews revealed that people assign significant intrinsic value to respect and view it as a form of social capital. Respect is the quality that people want most. In short, it changes the game.

A number of supporting research findings corroborate my conviction that respect is the number 1 reason people love their workplace. For instance, in a survey of nearly 20,000 employees around the world, people who said their leaders treated them with respect were 55 percent more engaged.[2] Another survey conducted by the Society for Human Resources Management (SHRM) in 2014 demonstrated that respectful treatment of "all employees at all levels" was rated as "very important" by 72 percent of employees, making it the top overall ingredient of job satisfaction. And respect not only keeps us engaged, it makes us more effective. Work by leadership and change expert and author John Kotter, for instance, found that respect helps us achieve buy-in for ideas, win over dissenters, and enhance our credibility.[3]

It makes sense that respect drives engagement and performance, but what is respect really? I would argue it is different for each of us. In the abstract, employees want to work in an environment where they feel appreciated, trusted, and listened to—a workplace that is fair, inclusive, and supportive. As part of that, *respect* can be defined as consideration for self and of others.[4] In action, respect can be seen in things like delivering on promises, walking the talk, and treating people as you would like to be

WHY RESPECT IS THE EC SPARK

Respect ⟶ systemic collaboration because people who respect each other work more effectively and efficiently together.

Respect ⟶ positive future because respect delivers the optimism people need to innovate and feel upbeat about the future for themselves and their organization.

Respect ⟶ alignment of values when mutual respect is a core value across the organization. Studies show that people who feel respected are more likely to show respect for others.

Respect ⟶ killer achievement when respect delivers the confidence and psychological safety that helps set people up to succeed.

treated. For some, that means the boss keeps them in the loop, gives them credit for their accomplishments, and doesn't micromanage. For others, it means working on a team with people who don't take their effort and expertise for granted. Still others think of respect as a high level of civility running across the organization consistently. Whatever the exact definition, respect connects us to each other and helps us work together better to achieve more.

We will look at some of the important elements of respect and how to put them into practice in the Best Practices Playbook below, but in the meantime, it is just as important to understand why respect is so difficult to build into the culture of an organization and why it is so hard to recapture once it is lost.

The Barriers: When Respect Is Withheld

When I enter an organization to assist in a cultural intervention, I start by taking the temperature. As part of that, I meet with people at every level to ask about workplace situations that concern and irritate them. Some of the answers I commonly hear are these: "My manager cancels our performance discussions without notice." "My colleague talks over me in meetings." "My team members call me at home at all hours of the night." These are vastly dissimilar issues, but they all come down to respect or the lack thereof.

Respect is something we either choose to give or withhold. The reason it is such a difficult issue is not because organizations are so complex but because people themselves are. From my experience, the issue of respect usually boils down to one of two dimensions: difference or dysfunction.

The first—*difference*—is not something that we can or should "solve." The accelerating pace of change and technology speeds up interactions and introduces new situations into the mix among diverse cultures and demographics. Even if we believe deeply in the basic tenets of respect, differences based on mindset, culture, and context can drive a wedge between people or cause individuals to act in ways that others find offensive, insulting, or disrespectful.

Differences in mindset, for instance, can create a dynamic whereby two people looking at the same situation reach opposite conclusions. As the famous Myers-Briggs Type Indicator (MBTI) and other personality assessments show, there are multiple ways people respond to conflict, stress, and interpersonal dynamics. Similarly, *type A and type B personality theory*, created by a pair of cardiologists in the 1950s, highlights opposing archetypes. Type A individuals are the ambitious high achievers that the researchers associated with a "high risk of heart disease." In contrast, type B individuals are more laid-back, deliberate, and even tempered.[5] The point is, when you put opposing personalities together at work, differences in style and thinking lead to conflicts and potentially to a lack of respect that is either real or perceived. What is important when dealing with people's differences is acknowledging the range of diversity and not excusing bad or abusive behavior based on nuances in style or mindset.

The other element that characterizes disrespect in the workplace is *dysfunction*. This term may refer to a toxic work environment where people act out, shout, intimidate, or belittle each other or take advantage of other abusive power plays. This type of bad behavior decimates trust, demoralizes teams, and leads to widespread burnout. Of the toxic behavior that is most insidious, bullying takes the cake because it remains in the shadows, and it disproportionately affects minority workers.[6] What's more, it can come from anywhere— bullying bosses are just as common as despicable or disrespecting colleagues.

Workplace bullying is abusive behavior that creates an intimidating or humiliating working environment with the purpose or effect of harming others' dignity, safety, and well-being.[7] It can be a power play or any similar dynamic where the "stronger" person preys on someone physically or emotionally weaker, or it can be a group that outnumbers a minority of individuals.

A Tokyo-based CEO and executive coach I know told me about the type of abusive behavior that is present in some Japanese corporations. He said that what we might consider bullying is commonplace in the Japanese workplace (as well as Japanese schools) because the culture prizes sameness and conformity over difference and individuality. In addition, he said, weakness is "severely frowned upon," and oftentimes it is verbally derided.

"Bullying [in Japan] is a way to coax people into conformity with longstanding cultural norms," he said. "The phrase *kireru* is the type of common abuse of authority that occurs when managers belittle and harshly criticize people in front of other employees."

Whether it is a culture that has come to condone bullying or a toxic workplace that tolerates harassment, this type of blatant disrespect is worth noting because it is the antithesis of what Howard Schultz and Howard Behar were trying to create at Starbucks and the opposite of the culture of connectedness that characterizes the In Great Company approach.

As I will show below, creating a culture of respect includes setting rules, speaking up, and setting an example that inspires engagement, empathy, and inclusion.

Respect: The Best Practices Playbook

Wegmans, the East Coast supermarket chain, is an excellent example of an operation that has given its all to create and sustain a culture of respect. With 98 stores and 58,000 employees, the family-owned organization is famously people centric, and it has landed on *Fortune*'s annual list of 100 Best Companies to Work For every year since the list first appeared, including earning the number 2 spot in 2018.

The company's approach is simple but distinctive: listen to employees, support their development and growth, acknowledge their personal lives and individual needs—repeat. Both Wegmans and Starbucks have followed this formula. And these people-centric practices are a part of several larger ideals that create a culture of respect and a virtuous circle that keeps people emotionally connected (Figure 6.1).

1. Make Respect Mutual

Creating a culture based on mutual respect is everyone's responsibility: founders, executives, middle managers, line workers—all of us. It

FIGURE 6.1

needs to be intentionally orchestrated, purposefully managed, and sustained through consistent actions and enforcement of cultural norms.

The first clue about how Wegmans has been able to create a culture of mutual respect can be seen in its crystal clear corporate values. Out of five values, three are about empowering people and treating them well, and one is specific to respect:

- We care about the well-being and success of every person.
- High standards are a way of life. We pursue excellence in everything we do.
- We make a difference in every community we serve.
- We respect and listen to our people.
- We empower our people to make decisions that improve their work and benefit our customers and our company.

Wegmans's counterintuitive mantra—"Employees First, Customers Second"—is further proof that the organization is prepared to stake its reputation on treating people well.

"Our employees are our number 1 asset, period," Kevin Stickles, the company's vice president for human resources, said in the *Atlantic*. "The first question you ask is: 'Is this the best thing for the employee?' That's a totally different model."[8]

More than just words on a page, this people-first policy is put into practice. For example, the organization earmarks millions each year ($50 million in 2017) for employee development,[9] including leadership training and tuition assistance programs. According to the company, more than half of their managers have worked with the store since high school or college, and many completed their education with help from Wegmans scholarship assistance program."[10]

The company also shows respect by listening to employees. They make a point to be transparent about business practices and ask employees to weigh in on improvements and new business initiatives.[11] (According to SHRM, when deli employees said the "cut gloves" they used with meat slicers were less than ideal, the company got further feedback and then provided custom-made gloves that addressed employee concerns.[12]) Finally, they demonstrate respect for people's personal needs by building flexibility into scheduling hours and offering people-first perks like adoption assistance.[13]

An institutional focus on respect has a viral effect when employees return the love. They respect the organization, each other, and the customers they serve. By all indications, this is the case with Wegmans. According to a report from the Temkin Group, Wegmans's customer service outranks that of any other company, regardless of industry, and a separate survey of 12,700 shoppers found that Wegmans is America's favorite grocery store, scoring 77 percent on its customer loyalty index.[14]

"When you think about employees first, the bottom line is better," Stickles argued in the *Atlantic*. "We want our employees to extend the brand to our customers."[15]

This sounds a lot like what Howard Behar told me about the big benefits of respect: "Grow the people, the people grow the organization, the organization grows the business. And that's how it works," he said.

Let's look at several related ways to make respect mutual.

Pass the Trust Test

Trust is a core component of respect that is entirely worth cultivating. The payback in high-trust companies is lower stress, higher productivity, fewer sick days, elevated engagement, and greater job satisfaction.[16] And like respect, trust must be mutual in order to deliver on its promise to engage and connect us. Each leader, team member, and individual needs to be believable, dependable, and focused on common goals. In other words, people need to do what they say they will. If there is a gap between what people say and what they actually do, then trust breaks down over time, and the ties between them become tenuous.

In my trust-building work within organizations I coach people to focus their efforts in a few ways. First, empower people to work in ways they want to. If people are in the right roles, they will know how to best do their job without overly tight oversight. Second, create a workplace that provides the resources and information people need to succeed. Withholding or hoarding facts, data, or even advice and coaching destroys trust and diminishes performance. Finally, take relationships seriously. Trust is a bond between and among people. The more we get to know each other, the better we understand the other's strengths and needs, and the stronger the bonds between us become. These gestures of trust each do two important things: they demonstrate trust, and they elicit trust in return. With that, they help forge the mutual trust that respect requires.

Create a Culture of Civility

One of the main reasons people provide for being rude and uncivil at work is time constraints. They are in a hurry, late, behind schedule, or otherwise time starved. As a result, they exhibit rude or ill-tempered behavior that sows discord in the workplace. A second everyday reason people provide for incivility? Personal issues. They are preoccupied with life's events or problems at home, and they carry their stress and negativity with them into the office.

From where I stand, these common justifications for disrespect are poor excuses for the garden variety incivility that, if left unchecked, can lead to more extreme bad behavior such as bullying and belittling. Before long, employees are treating customers with disrespect as well. Conversely, the workplaces that are role models of respect have a very low tolerance for incivility.

At Starbucks, for example, "it was almost impossible to get fired for missing your numbers. But if you treated people with disrespect, we would talk to you and coach you, . . . but if it became a pattern, you were going to be gone," Behar said. "That was the quickest way out the door because that's what mattered most to us."

The best way to create a culture of civility is to model it from the top down. When leaders are even tempered and able to treat people in a polite manner, it trickles down. And 360-degree feedback is the best tool to hold people at all levels accountable. Basic respect matters enough to people that it will come out if you include the right questions as part of routine management assessments.

Creating a baseline of civility is so important, in part, because it is simple. If it falls to the wayside, much more gets destroyed with it, and suddenly incivility is simply a symptom of a much larger problem.

Put Fairness First

Fairness is yet another pillar of respect, and it manifests in many very different ways: rewarding people justly for their accomplishments, treating them well when they are leaving or laid off, keeping an open mind and withholding blame when something goes wrong, giving them airtime when a decision will affect them, holding everyone accountable for the same rules, and rewarding people equally, and so on.

Many times, we can enable fairness simply by putting processes in place to ensure that everyone is treated similarly and justly with transparent due process. What are the milestones for promotion? How many months' severance do people receive? What is the family leave policy? If everyone knows the rules around these and other issues—and the policy is fair and just—it will cut down on people feeling that they have been treated unfairly.

Acting consistently and fairly is not always the easiest or the fastest way to do things, but it is the most respectful, and it will pay dividends in engagement, productivity, and loyalty.

2. Respect Differences

Inclusion is about trust, civility, and fairness all rolled into one. It is arguably the single biggest facet of respect and perhaps the most important to organizational success and emotional connectedness. *Inclusion*, which I define as active, intentional, and ongoing engagement with diversity and the commitment to treat people fairly and value them equally regardless of their differences, has proven over and again to be good for bottom-line business and great for engagement.

As a recent McKinsey study shows, "Companies in the top quartile for racial and ethnic diversity are 35 percent more likely to have financial returns above their respective national industry medians."[17] In addition, a separate study showed that diverse companies had higher cash flow per employee over a three-year period than nondiverse companies.[18] Findings like this abound.

Inclusion has worked for Wegmans, just as it has for so many other organizations. The grocer's proactive stance on diversity landed it at number 8 on the *Forbes* list of America's Best Employers for Diversity in 2018.[19]

Yet, my favorite example of inclusion as a lever for emotional connectedness is the Girl Scouts of the USA under the leadership of the remarkable Frances Hesselbein. During her 24 years at Girl Scouts, including 14 as CEO, Hesselbein mobilized a critical turnaround for the organization. During her tenure, membership quadrupled, diversity more than tripled, and the organization was transformed into what Peter Drucker called "the best-managed organization around." Hesselbein accomplished the amazing turnaround with a paid staff of 6,000 and a volunteer staff of 730,000.[20]

"To start, we studied ourselves and found that we were not nearly as representative as we needed to be," Hesselbein told me.[21] She enlisted Vernon Jordan, then president of the National Urban League, and Robert Hill, the noted sociologist, researcher, and advocate for African American equality and civil rights, to help identify ways the club could start to appeal to minority girls. Yet, changing a 106-year-old organization with a rigidly established culture and traditional values is far easier said than done. At the time, the organization was designed to draw the vast majority of its members from white middle-class America.

Hesselbein said the real inaugural step to change was envisioning a more inclusive future. "When you have a vision designed to ignite a vast and multicultural organization, and when you have a clear, powerful statement of why you must transform, it's amazing how you can take the lead and move right into the future and give other people the courage to do the same," she said.

One of the most important, and exceedingly challenging, aspects of the change process was updating the organization's powerful touchstones—the ubiquitous Girl Scout pin and the iconic *Girl Scout Handbook*.

About the pin, she said, "Here we had 788,000 adults in the organization, and we had used this pin and this logo since 1912. How do you move into the future without alienating or having people feel they're part of the past, and yet you know you have to be part of the future?"

Hesselbein acknowledged and addressed the challenge and moved ahead with resolve. About the updated pin, which depicted three diverse female faces looking out toward the future, she said: "When any little girl or young woman in the United States looks at the pin, she must find herself." And the handbook: "If I'm a little girl on a Navaho reservation, I should be able to open my Brownie handbook and see myself there."

Hesselbein succeeded in transforming the Girl Scouts and leading the organization to a new, more diverse era of dynamic success. *It was that repetition in the storytelling, consistency of messaging, and Hesselbein's ability to envision the change that was called for that made her so powerful as a leader and change maker.* She was awarded the Presidential Medal of Freedom in 1998 in part for her work in Girl Scouts.

Hesselbein's example is as instructive as it is inspiring, and hers is one of the stories that illustrates the prescriptions that follow that make inclusion a main lever for unleashing respect within organizations of any type.

Dig Deeper with Data

Having a rigorous process in place to measure and monitor inclusion is a cornerstone of success. Without systematic transparency and dedicated resources and effort, inclusion can quickly fall to the wayside.

At the beginning of her transformation of the Girl Scouts, Frances Hesselbein used a process to measure their current level of inclusion and set an ambitious goal for the future. Many notably inclusive organizations have since taken this best practice to an even higher level. The Australian enterprise software firm Atlassian, for instance, mentioned in Chapter 3, is known for its unusually in-depth analysis and reporting on inclusion and diversity within its workforce. For its part, Atlassian delivers data on inclusion not only at the aggregate corporate level but also at the individual team level, so the organization and their stakeholders can see how inclusion plays out across all groups. This state-of-the-art reporting sets the standard for the tech industry and creates a benchmark for Atlassian's competitors to match.[22]

Detailed transparency into diverse representation within your workforce makes it possible to get beyond generalities to measure representation on teams, in roles, and around the leadership table.

View Inclusion Broadly

In practice, inclusion on teams should go beyond statistical multicultural diversity. The governing norms and workplace environment needs to be such that people feel safe and able to participate and be themselves. In particular, people need to feel free to disagree and even dissent.

Dominic Barton, global managing partner for McKinsey & Company, takes this idea even further, saying, "One of our most important values is the obligation to dissent. Which means not only do you have the right to say, 'I disagree with you,' or 'I don't like that piece of thinking,' or 'I don't like the way you're approaching this or how you're talking to me,' or whatever, but you must say it."[23]

Honest dissent and truth telling are both forms of respect in a functioning meritocracy, Barton told me.

Hesselbein put this idea into practice at the Girl Scouts as a means for engaging people in the change effort. She allowed local councils to make their own decision in the beginning about which pin and logo design to order, for example. "Doing this is a key principle in managing change and mobilizing people around it," she explained. "If you act in a dismissive way when people oppose you, they will never support the change, but if you give them time, attention, and your genuine respect, it creates a tremendous amount of goodwill."

We get far more emotional connectedness from the inclusion imperative if all ideas and ways of thinking are represented and taken into account and when people feel able to authentically participate and dissent.

Make Inclusion Mission Critical

Inclusion needs to be a core value in organizations—thereby going beyond a human resources or compliance purview and making it everyone's priority. Yet, it needs to be built into the fabric of business as well.

Hesselbein knew that expanding the Girl Scouts' appeal beyond white middle-class members to include the full range of diversity in America was the only way the organization would survive. It was a values imperative, to be sure, but it was also a business priority. The more ways we can build inclusion into all parts of organizations from culture to commerce, the faster it takes hold as a way to connect us to each other and the organization.

3. Lead with Respect

If we look at the CEOs who have the highest Glassdoor ratings, respect comes up over and over again as one of the key factors for their success.[24] Unfortunately, research also shows that 54 percent of employees have said they don't receive the respect they need from leaders.[25]

Given the dominant workforce trends, leading with respect is especially important going forward. First, as organizations become less hierarchical, flatter, and more team based, leaders rotate in and out of roles, come into contact with many different types of people, and need to operate within a paradigm of empowerment. Respect is a key leadership trait that makes flat or matrixed organizations operate more smoothly.

Next, leaders can't hide behind their mahogany desks or rely on middle managers to interact with frontline employees. With social networks and myriad new channels of communication connecting us to each other, leaders are required to interact regularly and respectfully with employees as a way to engage and inspire them. Finally, it is no secret that millennials and younger workers, like many generations before them, are looking for jobs that matter more and match their values. As part of that, they expect leaders to communicate transparently, use influence as opposed to pure authority, and act based on trust as opposed to job title. In short, respect has become a leadership imperative.

Yet, while the leadership paradigm has changed, not all leaders understand the shift. Many still operate in command-and-control mode where showing respect is either optional for leaders or reserved for their executive peers. The reasons are varied. Some leaders are not self-aware enough to know when they are acting with disrespect; others are too busy to offer the recognition and appreciation that employees associate with respect; still others are the type of toxic leaders that leave people running for the exits the first chance they get.

Regardless of the reason, leaders need to see that respect matters most. Throughout this book, I take the perspective that being In Great Company is a collective effort, and emotional connectedness matters to everyone. But the fact remains: if leaders don't exhibit respect, they won't receive it in return. When organizations operate based on fear instead of respect, people don't give their best, and they withhold loyalty. Luckily, the opposite is also true. When employees respect leaders, it establishes trust and keeps people committed and connected.

As an executive coach, I work one-on-one with leaders to help them make the changes they need to be successful. In this case, helping leaders to see the powerful role respect plays in emotional connectedness comes down to a few actions, described below, that have more to do with mindset than systems or structure.

Practice Self-Awareness

Toxic leadership aside, most of us want to project respect, but we face hidden barriers within ourselves. Some of us are slightly disconnected from reality, and we don't realize how others perceive our behavior. Others are accustomed to being treated with deference, and they are thrown off when someone speaks the truth or dissents. Most often? When we act in a disrespectful manner, it is because we don't fully respect ourselves.

The leadership psyche is complicated, and most of us are clueless about the things that trigger our bad behavior. This is where self-awareness comes in. In his bestselling book *Emotional Intelligence*, psychologist Daniel Goleman defines *self-awareness* as "knowing one's internal states, preferences, resources, and intuitions."[26] If that sounds esoteric and unimportant, it's not. A 2010 study by the Cornell School of Industrial and Labor Relations found self-awareness to be the strongest predictor of overall success in leaders.[27] It makes intuitive sense. Self-awareness helps us play to our strengths, understand our fatal flaws, and surround ourselves with people who can fill in the gaps.

Pursuing honest self-reflection aimed at isolating our development needs is a proactive endeavor. Luckily, most companies offer multiple opportunities for executives to get to know themselves, hear the feedback they need, and begin to see what motivates their decision-making and behavior. Executive coaching is one common path to help leaders reach enlightenment. Others are 360-degree feedback and leadership assessments. The easiest way? Ask people you trust to tell you the truth about how you are perceived—and listen to them. Leaders who can get to the root cause of their problem with respect are in a position to solve it before it does irreparable damage to their reputation and relationships.

I put it this way to leaders: pursue self-awareness as if your career depended on it, because it does.

Communicate Your Respect

There are numerous ways for leaders to signal respect. As we will see in the next section, it is often the little things that mean the most to people—making eye contact, thanking them for their help, remembering their names, and countless other intimate gestures. However, I would argue that communication in general is not a little thing. It's everything when it comes to demonstrating your respect.

Garry Ridge, CEO of WD-40, is a big believer in communication as a tool to truly connect with the 450 "tribe members" at the company. In an interview, Ridge said, "Communication doesn't come in one flavor. The key to communication is the permission to communicate. There are four things that come into play here: care, candidacy, accountability, and responsibility. I care about my people. I take a deep interest in who they are and what they do. I consistently take initiatives to make them feel cared for. Ultimately, communication is all about consistency."[28]

Communication means a lot to Ridge, and he is an expert at engaging with his tribe in an impactful and positive way. How does Ridge let employees know that he respects them and their needs? He encourages them to reach out to him directly with concerns, and he responds within 24 hours.[29]

Communication is at the core of human relationships, and it is the greatest tool leaders have to lead with respect and create a workplace that keeps people coming back.

4. The Small Things Are Big

Dr. Terry Jackson, noted author and executive coach, shared his experience leading the turnaround of a multibillion-dollar business. It was a massive challenge, and Jackson needed to gain as much knowledge as he could before beginning. Some leaders in his position would do a deep dive into the numbers, examine future objectives and corporate history, and stop there. But Jackson went further. He sat down with all of the employees individually to hear about their professional and personal goals, and he listened to as much as they were willing to share about themselves. He collected data on their birthdays, wedding anniversaries, the names and birthdays of their spouses and children, and even the names of their pets. His approach was designed to demonstrate his genuine interest in every person and to make the emotional connection that would give them a better chance to succeed.

"The ultimate objective was to improve people's engagement and drive increased productivity, which would deliver increased sales, revenue, and profit," he said. "On a deeper level, I believed that their success was also my success. If I cleared the obstacles, they could do what they do best: close deals that generate revenue."[30]

Using small gestures to demonstrate respect and gratitude, Jackson showed people that they mattered to the organization. For instance, for five years straight, they sent congratulatory e-mails, birthday cards, and anniversary messages to everyone in the company. Jackson himself delivered handwritten messages congratulating people on personal and professional achievements.

These small gestures made all the difference. Revenue in the division tripled in less than five years, everyone on the team at one point made the prestigious Century Club (an all-expense-paid company trip for top performers), and in 2011 Jackson himself was named best division director in the organization.

"We turned around performance and engagement," Jackson said. "Ours became the division where everyone wanted to work."

Jackson's story is unusual and inspiring, but it is not necessarily surprising. Science supports the idea that small gestures are the secret sauce of respect. For example, researchers at King's College in London and the Yale Center for Emotional Intelligence used magnetic resonance imaging (MRI) to study the effects of specific emotions on people's limbic system, a complex bundle of nerves and networks in the brain that affect mood and manage basic emotions like fear and pleasure. They found that social connectedness emerges from feelings of gratitude and appreciation—both are elements of respect.

All of this tells us that we need to see organizations for what they truly are—collections of people. People want to be understood and acknowledged. We can easily offer this to people, simply by focusing on the little things that really matter to them. The following are a few of the things that add up to the respect that people want and expect.

Go Heavy on Gratitude

Saying thank you is one of the best things we can do for the people we work with, and it does wonders for business. One study by Glassdoor found that 80 percent of employees would be willing to work harder for an appreciative boss, and 70 percent said they'd feel better about themselves and their efforts if their boss thanked them more regularly.[31]

This simple symbol of respect has more impact than almost any other in creating emotional connectedness. Former Campbell Soup CEO Doug Conant put this practice into action starting in 2001, when he was brought on to turn around the organization at a time when it was in decline and "reeling from a series of layoffs."[32] Over the course of his tenure at Campbell's, Conant wrote 30,000 thank-you notes to employees for everything from major accomplishments to small acts of kindness. Needless to say, Conant left the organization in far better shape than it was in when he arrived.

This same custom worked for former Home Depot CEO Frank Blake. During his seven years as CEO, he set aside time every Sunday to hand-write thank-you notes to employees. He estimates he wrote more than 25,000. And when Blake retired in 2017, employees returned the favor: Blake received hundreds of appreciative notes from Home Depot associates.[33]

There are limitless ways we can express gratitude in the workplace. Some organizations have literally institutionalized gratitude by making it a stated policy to thank people after particularly labor-intensive projects or accomplishments. Other companies list gratitude as part of their corporate values and make a point to build it into their business. But most companies that put gratitude to great use simply make it customary to thank each other as often as possible.

Gratitude can exist everywhere in the organization. Far from being just a job for leaders, it can come from the top down, bottom up, and everywhere else in the organization.

Consider the Human Experience

Part of respect is acknowledging the human condition and empathizing with what people are dealing with in their personal lives outside work.

Making a habit of being empathetic is simple and involves some of the steps I prescribe throughout this book. First, listen to people without judging. You'll never truly empathize with anyone unless you can pause long enough to earnestly learn something about their hopes, fears, and unique circumstances. Next, put yourself in their shoes. It only takes a moment to try to imagine how someone else feels. Finally, do something that shows your empathy: express interest, make a caring remark, offer an idea, or share a similar story of your own.

Empathy is especially impactful when organizations act in a manner that has a positive impact on their employees' personal lives. One of the ways Wegmans takes people's lives into account is by making it easy for them to manage their work schedule in a flexible way. Their system allows workers to choose their own shifts to accommodate things like doctors' appointments, dependent sick days, and children's school breaks.

Empathetic behavior shows people that they are being heard and understood. Respecting people's lives in this way makes them feel appreciated, and it brings us together around that one thing that all of us have in common: we're human.

RESPECT: EXECUTIVE SUMMARY

Positive Best Practices	Ground Rules
Make respect mutual.	Pass the trust test. Create a culture of civility. Put fairness first.
Respect differences.	Dig deeper with data. View inclusion broadly. Make inclusion mission critical.
Lead with respect.	Practice self-awareness. Communicate your respect.
The small things are big.	Go heavy on gratitude. Consider the human experience.

CHAPTER 7

KILLER ACHIEVEMENT

Killer achievement happens when CEOs and companies create support systems, cultures, and structures that set people up to succeed. With this, they become so emotionally connected with colleagues and customers that success becomes sustainable, self-reinforcing, and almost a force all its own.

Reed Hastings knows a little something about killer achievement. As cofounder and CEO of the streaming and entertainment frontrunner Netflix, the entrepreneur and philanthropist launched the service in 1989 as a movie-by-mail upstart opposite Blockbuster's bustling brick-and-mortar monolith. Given the two firms' overlapping interests, Hastings proposed a marketing partnership with Blockbuster in 2000: Netflix would manage the online marketing of both brands, and Blockbuster would promote Netflix in its stores. Blockbuster's marketing team reportedly laughed Hastings right out the door. You know the rest. Blockbuster went belly up in 2010, and Netflix walked off with the category.

As of 2018, the company that started with 900 movie rentals has since evolved into an algorithm-driven behemoth that has viewers binge watching 70,000 streaming offerings, including its own Oscar-winning content. In 2017, Netflix raked in more than $11 billion in revenue, and the company had 125 million subscribers.[1] How did Netflix make the astounding shift from being America's most misunderstood and undervalued company[2] to becoming number 10 on LinkedIn's Best Places to Work list in 2018? By developing and scaling a strong culture of achievement.

Netflix's achievement-driven people strategy is captured in an infamous and unusual 125-page Slideshare document that has become known as "the culture deck."[3] Viewed 18 million times online and passed around HR and leadership circles, the culture deck is deliberately provocative and boils down to two words: *freedom* and *responsibility*.

A few proof points that typify Netflix's culture of achievement: Salaried employees can take as many paid days off as they want (freedom), but they are expected to consistently perform at a high level and exceed expectations (responsibility). They have few spending controls or travel and expense limitations (freedom), but they are expected to make spending decisions that are "in Netflix's best interests" (responsibility). The organization has eliminated all performance reviews (freedom), but the company uses a simple and informal 360-feedback system where anyone can provide feedback to anyone else in the company (responsibility).

Here are some of the other highlights from the original culture deck:

▶ Instead of a culture of process adherence, they have a culture of "creativity and self-discipline."

▶ Netflix leaders hire, develop, and cut smartly so they "have stars in every position."

▶ They "help each other to be great."

▶ "They don't measure people by how many hours they work but by great work accomplished."[4]

Sheryl Sandberg has called the culture deck one of the most important documents ever to come out of Silicon Valley.[5] Why? Because it is a big part of Netflix's success paradigm. And although the company's specific focus on superstars and uber-achievers is not for everyone (merely "adequate" performers receive a "generous severance package"[6]), they are on to something here. The idea of enabling achievement came up over and over again in my research. It turns out that working toward a common goal brings people together. Most of us are happier when clear goals and accountability markers are put onto place, and we are surrounded by like-minded achievers. People crave uninterrupted progress, and they want to dedicate themselves to a larger purpose. Even more, they want organizations to eliminate systemic and practical barriers to achievement so they can feel fulfilled and be their best to help drive success.

Why Achievement Is So Satisfying

Many of us have been raised to believe that working hard to achieve our life's goals will deliver all the happiness we need. And it's true in a sense. But it's not any single achievement that keeps us satisfied over the long term. Instead, it's several different dynamics of achievement that come together to delight and engage us at work and in our lives.

The first is *goal setting*. Research shows that goal setting positively affects employee engagement and individual performance. Even more, one study found that goal setting is part of a virtuous chain: goal setting in organizations positively affects employee engagement, employee engagement positively affects optimism, and optimism positively affects individual performance.[7] What part of goal setting is particularly uplifting? Envisioning a positive view of ourselves—aspiration is motivational. Yet, the key to connecting goal setting with engagement is the balance between creating stretch goals that inspire and motivate people while also keeping the goals realistic.

The second positive dynamic in achievement is *progress.* A study in the *Journal of Happiness Studies* showed that making progress toward our goals might just bring as much satisfaction as actually achieving them.[8] We mentioned the positive impact of progress in Chapter 4, "Positive Future," but the point bears repeating: progress is emotionally fulfilling. According to author and behavioral psychologist Dan Ariely, most of us thrive by making constant progress and feeling the sense of purpose that goes along with it.[9] Similar research shows that breaking major goals into smaller steps that we achieve along the way is similarly uplifting, in part because it delivers a pulse of positive hormones every time we achieve a small win.[10]

Emotional connectedness is the other element that comes into play here. The sense of satisfaction that is derived from shared purpose and team support affects achievement. For example, we experience emotional connectedness when we work together with others to achieve a common goal. And publicly sharing our progress with others can actually help motivate us to accomplish our goals.[11] Of course, the bump in achievement from group interactions is more likely to have the desired effect when we receive positive support and constructive feedback.

Finally, it worth noting that ample recent research demonstrates a different type of connection between achievement and happiness. In this case, it's happiness that drives the achievement.

We are more effective, creative, and collaborative when we are happy at work.[12]

Achievement, then, is actually a set of behaviors and reciprocal dynamics, not a single event or a moment in time. In other words, the joy is in the journey. Netflix employees love their workplace— not because they logged 9 million or more new subscribers in any particular quarter, but because the company sets ambitious but attainable goals that motivate people to work toward them as a team.

The Achievement Gap: Barriers to Success

In 2003, I conducted a survey of nurses across America to determine what actions motivated high achievement and what conditions created the opposite effect.[13] The primary complaint most nurses cited had nothing to do with compensation or patient outcome. Instead, the nurses reported feeling undervalued and underappreciated. Although they spent far more of their time supporting individual patients, they were not given proper respect or adequate credit for their work by the doctors. This left them feeling demoralized and unfulfilled.

There are dozens of reasons why some organizations can create environments where people are set up to succeed while other companies sink into disarray and dysfunction. Many causes are specific to individual people—they are in the wrong roles or stuck in a career rut—but other issues are common across industries. From my experience, the achievement gap is almost always the result of a misalignment of expectations.

Like the nurses in my survey, a lack of recognition in organizations creates a misalignment between what people think they deserve and what they receive. Cultures that fail to recognize hard work, lionize one job and marginalize another, or fail to properly align achievement with incentives, all lose their best people to disappointment and burnout. I call this the *expectation/reward misalignment.*

Another common mismatch is the *experience/skills misalignment.* When industries shift due to emerging technologies and changing business models, it leaves large segments of their workforce without the skills they need to achieve. In industries like telecom, energy, and even manufacturing, trends such as digital and mobile technology, sustainability, and artificial intelligence are all changing faster than individual workers can retrain. This leaves companies with talent gaps and people with no way to perform up to their potential.

A third disconnect that impacts achievement is the *goals/systems misalignment.* This occurs when goals are beyond reach due to any number of limitations ranging from resources and organizational structure to "head count." Although stretch goals have worked wonders for companies like Google, 3M, Apple, and Boeing, these organizations give individuals the resources, training, and creative latitude to achieve the seemingly impossible.[14] In other cases, the unintended consequences of the goals/systems misalignment run the gamut from disengagement at the personal level, when people can't deliver, to risky behavior on an institutional scale. In the financial services environment, for example, when marketing goals far surpass staffing levels and regulatory limitations, it periodically leads to illegal and unethical behavior as rules and laws are disregarded in order to meet supersized sales expectations.

Each of these misalignments makes it impossible for people to succeed and organizations to reach their peak achievement. Sometimes the disappointment goes viral, and it sends the company into a tailspin. In the Best Practices Playbook below, I will describe practical and logistical fixes that address these barriers and imbalances to create a culture of connection that sets people up to achieve.

Killer Achievement:
The Best Practices Playbook

In 2012, it seemed like Best Buy was headed for the same retail graveyard where Circuit City ended its run. As with so many other defunct electronics retailers, the formerly bustling megastore had been dragged down by plummeting profits and what is known in retail as *showrooming*: customers pack into stores to get a feel for high-end products only to head outside to buy the item on Amazon for less. Best Buy failed to make a critical strategic shift in its business, and the ensuing misalignment was nearly fatal. To make matters worse, their chief executive was given the ax under a cloud of scandal and named "Worst CEO of 2012" by CNBC.

Yet, Best Buy clearly had some fight left in it. According to Spencer Stuart's Jim Citrin, who led the search for a new CEO, "There was a deep reservoir of passion within Best Buy employees. They had been winners and innovators in the past, but now a critical piece was missing."[15]

So, what was missing? A leader with a vibrant vision to reignite passion in employees and a core strategy that would enable achievement. Enter Hubert Joly. Despite initial skepticism from some industry analysts, Joly leveraged his experience in global hospitality, travel, and entertainment—and he turned out to be the complete package. He had the requisite turnaround experience, service mentality, and technology savvy. And above all, Citrin said, he was "a great strategic thinker" who was "committed to culture and building an environment to get the best people motivated and moving in the right direction."

In the Best Practices Playbook below, I will outline how to use the killer achievement element to spark emotional connection, just as Best Buy and other high-performance organizations have (Figure 7.1).

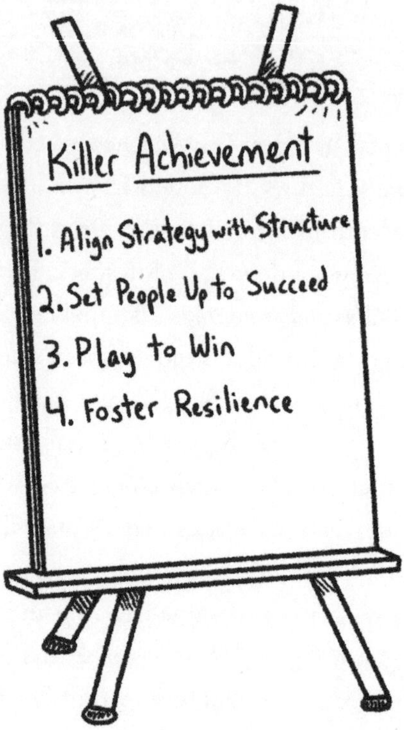

FIGURE 7.1

1. Align Strategy with Structure

Under Joly's lead, Best Buy strengthened its website while also making crucial improvements at the store level. For example, they began matching Amazon's prices. That empowered "sales associates at stores to close more sales, and it gave customers a reason to purchase products on the spot rather than ordering online" from Amazon and waiting for the shipment. On their website, they improved search and checkout capabilities, among other things. The new strategy—called "Renew Blue"—suited the shifting industry dynamics whereby customers wanted low prices and an enhanced customer experience online and off. By eliminating the barriers to success, employees were able to focus on achievement. The result?

By 2017, sales were strong, and the company announced that its turnaround was complete, and it was moving into a growth phase.

Aligning strategy with structure unites people in service of a common objective and sets them free to achieve. Here are a few prescriptive lessons that Best Buy and other achievement-oriented companies have to offer that put this specific best practice into context in the workplace.

Balance Focus and Flexibility

Organizations need a stated strategic focus to rally their workforce around a common goal. At the same time, they need to empower people to remain flexible and respond to change.

During their critical turnaround phase, Joly and Best Buy "resisted the temptation to chase shiny objects."[16] Their sights were fixed on reshaping the business by partnering with many of the foremost tech experts. For example, between 2013 and 2018, they carved partnerships with vendors including Samsung (mobile, TV, appliances), Sony, Microsoft, Canon, Nikon, AT&T, Verizon, Google, and even Amazon, and they also they grew their relationship with Apple. In turn, these companies not only invested in Best Buy displays, but many of them also chipped in to invest in labor, training, and marketing at the retailer. (So, not only did these brands have a place to show off their products, but Best Buy sales associates also had a better understanding of their products—how they worked and how they worked with other products or within an ecosystem.)

At the same time, Best Buy scanned the periphery for emerging opportunities. One sign of flexibility amid the focus was an extension of the marketing partnership between Best Buy and Amazon that brought the organizations together to sell, exclusively, smart TVs equipped with Amazon's video streaming capabilities and the Alexa voice assistant. This combination of focus and flexibility signaled Best Buy's shift from turnaround artist to growth mode.

WD-40 is another company that uses the focus and flexibility mantra to enable achievement. While CEO Garry Ridge directs their efforts in smart support of their ubiquitous blue and yellow can, he also expects people to take risks, explore change, and look for growth opportunities. In fact, Ridge gives WD-40's employees a license to learn by insisting they uncover opportunities for the organization and its brand. As part of that, WD-40 employees take a "Maniac Pledge" to encourage ownership and experimentation: "I am responsible for taking action, asking questions, getting answers, and making decisions. I won't wait for someone to tell me. If I need to know, I am responsible for asking."[17]

Not unlike Netflix's freedom and responsibility imperative, the Maniac Pledge brings focus and flexibility together in a way that empowers people to achieve.

Communicate Goals Clearly

Aligning strategy and structure works best when objectives are simply stated and communicated repetitively. Simplicity like this makes goal alignment easier while repetition lights the path to achievement.

Best Buy focused their people around their Renew Blue strategy in a few ways. First, they clearly articulated the problems their turnaround plan was created to address: declining revenue and declining margin. Next, Joly, a McKinsey & Company alum, organized priorities around five succinct goals:

- Reinvigorate and rejuvenate the customer experience.
- Attract and inspire leaders and employees.
- Work with vendor partners to innovate and drive value.
- Increase return on invested capital (ROIC) for investors.

- Continue leadership role in positively affecting the world.[18]

Finally, the company managed progress carefully across the organization, always referring back to the original two problems. When they completed the turnaround in 2017, Joly was quick to communicate their next plan, called "New Blue." All of this consistency and simplicity made a complicated turnaround easier for people to rally around.

Even when a turnaround is not at stake, communicating goals effectively makes it easier to create a cascade effect whereby organizational and individual goals can be achieved in lockstep. *In my work with organizations, I've seen that simplicity means that employees can engage in goal setting and feedback opportunities in an effective way that focuses on meaningful achievement over mindless minutia.*

Set People Free to Achieve

The next way to align strategy and structure is to hire the right people and set them free to achieve. With focus and goal alignment as guardrails, then, people should be empowered to demonstrate all the confidence and creativity they need to succeed. For instance, the 125-page culture deck is effective at Netflix because it provides a way for people to proceed on their own as much as it guides them to understand the cultural imperative of freedom and responsibility. The creative software firm Adobe has a similar ethos. Employees are carefully screened and trained, and then they are assigned challenging projects and trusted to carry out their responsibilities without micromanagement.

Tom Kolditz has a complementary philosophy, drawn from his experience as a leader and teacher, that he calls "presumption of competence."[19]

"In an organizational context, 'presumption of competence' means you bring in people who are well trained and properly educated, who know the job, and you bestow a level of trust that helps them proceed and achieve," he said. "And when bad things happen or things run off course, the presumption is that it was a situational issue, not a personal one," he said.

The "presumption" is that the individuals involved are competent but the situation is flawed and can be addressed together. This presumption of competence lets smart people propose creative solutions and problem solve without fear of failure or finger pointing. It sets limits but also sets people free to achieve.

Channel Feedback for Achievement

Feedback is another important driver of achievement. As with positive future—where we need to plan for a positive future even as we solve problems and create a culture of accountability, feedforward comes into play again here. Although it is self-evident that feedback should align with goals, organizations are starting to see that the traditional assessment process actually hinders performance, so some are beginning to look for ways to change.

The biggest improvement is making feedback real time as opposed to waiting for the annual assessment. Adobe, for one, was an early adopter of redefining performance discussions to make them more meaningful to employees. Beginning in 2012, the organization has eliminated annual performance reviews, and it has scrapped archived paperwork and ranking. The company has replaced the process with regular discussions that cover expectations, feedback, and growth and development. The more informal, targeted discussions address performance issues *when they occur*, while experiences are fresh, instead of waiting for the review cycle, when employees and managers are left grasping for meaningful specifics that can affect future achievement.[20]

Google's approach is perhaps even more notable, and it dates back to the company's inception. Developed by venture capitalist John Doerr and described in his book, *Measure What Matters*, Google's performance management is built around setting and achieving audacious goals using *objectives and key results* (OKRs). The novel model gives organizations four "superpowers," including "focus and commit to priorities" and "track for accountability." The beauty in Google's approach is that it builds stretch goals and focused measurement into the daily fabric of the organization instead of using a historical approach that measures achievement instead of driving it.[21]

2. Set People Up to Succeed

People achieve more when organizations set them up to succeed through training, personal development, ongoing learning, and diverse opportunities to grow. Almost all of the leaders and executives I interviewed for this book mentioned ongoing learning and professional development as priority levers to help people at every level be their best. And research on employee engagement supports this. Learning opportunities, professional development, and career progression are among the top drivers of employee satisfaction and workforce success, according to Deloitte. As part of that, employees under the age of 35 rate professional development as their number 1 or number 2 driver of engagement.[22]

Jazz Pharmaceuticals, as well, put employee development directly at the center of their culture at a critical time for the organization. Eric Fink, Jazz CHRO, told me about creating the culture of learning and development that transformed the organization on the heels of the 2008 to 2009 recession. These are Fink's words:

> It was an especially dark moment for a lot of companies. Jazz was losing money, the stock was down to 53 cents a

share, and we were in default on our debt and closing in on bankruptcy. At the time, [CEO Bruce Cozadd] was trying to talk me into coming over to Jazz from Bayer to be head of learning and development. In the beginning I was thinking, why the heck are you hiring a sales trainer if you're considering going under? I had an infant just home after eight weeks in the neonatal intensive care unit (NICU) and another who was two years old. Why would my family and I pick up and move across the country to join a company on the edge of decline?

But the things that Bruce told me stuck with me. He wasn't telling me about hitting a certain stock price or winning over Wall Street at that point. He seemed far more passionate about building the culture of the company and setting us up to succeed.

He told me: "It's about the people. Do you know how we're going to rise up and out of this? By investing in our salespeople and getting them ready to drive revenues on our products. That's the plan. We're going to train people, and our employees will pull us out of this. We can do this together."

I flew back home after the meeting, and I couldn't let go of what he said. My mentors at the time were saying, "What the heck are you doing? You were at GSK [GlaxoSmithKline]. You wanted to go smaller, so you went to Bayer, which is a world-renowned pharmaceutical company, and now you're going to throw it all away and join some hundred-person company that's in financial freefall?"

But I was hooked. I was like, "I gotta do it. It's crazy, but I believe in this."

So we followed the plan and invested in people. We focused on training them, motivating them, and empowering them. And it worked. Over the next few years, we took a product that was approaching its 10-year anniversary, Xyrem, and elevated it from single-digit growth to double-digit-plus volume growth for three years running, which is unheard of. By that time, we were running on all cylinders in a number of ways and starting to look at new opportunities. Come 2012, we were paying our loans, we hit profitability, and we had cash in the bank. In a matter of two years we were in a completely different situation, largely driven by investing in people.[23]

Fink's story is unique, and he's passionate about learning, but the lesson itself applies across the board. Training and development set people up to succeed, and ongoing learning is one of the best ways to create the type of emotional connectedness that leads to peak achievement. Let's drill down into two of the best lessons.

Train Continuously

As we saw with Jazz Pharmaceuticals, learning is a cultural mandate as opposed to a single glitzy onboarding video or a one-off training session. It needs to be robust and continuous as a way to keep people engaged and connected—especially within large, complex companies that have technology as their backbone and constant transformation as the new normal.

This seems to be the perspective at Visa, where the organization continues to take its business forward by creating new ways to prepare global employees to support clients and partners as they migrate from plastic credit cards to digital payment options over multiple platforms. As part of that, Visa's learning and development (L&D) department took the lead to build a corporate university that included "physical learning hubs and a next-generation digital learning ecosystem . . . [that] brings all learning together [to] . . . develop skills they want and need to help them grow professionally."

The results look good so far. Six months after launch, more than 80 percent of the company's employees had interacted with the digital campus. Specifically, users started and/or completed formal learning or viewed and/or completed informal learning.[24]

AT&T is going through a similar talent transformation. It has partnered with Udacity and Georgia Tech to provide online courses and blended learning opportunities for over 140,000 employees to actively engage in acquiring new skills. Like Visa, AT&T is striving to create a culture of on-demand, ongoing learning.[25]

Make Learning Inclusive

The learning and career development programs at Visa and AT&T are vast and state of the art by necessity. Their businesses are built on technology that is changing rapidly, and their people need to be lifelong learners who constantly update their skills. Yet, even beyond technology companies, training needs to be accessible to everyone to yield emotional connectedness. This inclusion mandate is especially true in service-oriented industries where training has an immediate impact on customer satisfaction.

Nordstrom and Ritz-Carlton, both known for their gold standard employee training, have programs that are famously inclusive and immersive. In both cases, learning is built into the business every day. At Ritz-Carlton, for instance, employees at every location around the world have a daily huddle with managers before a shift begins, to talk about how to exemplify the culture and values of the organization.[26] The Cheesecake Factory, as well, provides learning opportunities across the board. Servers get two weeks of on-the-job training. Management candidates attend a 12-week development course. Even dishwashers are included in training initiatives.[27] And it has game-based training portals that include a "leaderboard" and an iPhone game.[28]

The result of inclusive training? The Cheesecake Factory, as well as Nordstrom and the Ritz-Carlton (as part of Marriott brands), are perennials on numerous best-places-to-work lists. As these organizations demonstrate, training and development opportunities set people up to succeed.

3. Play to Win

If alignment and training are critical to achievement, so too is mindset. *My research shows that people want to be part of an organization that plays to win because passion and dedication add more meaning to work.* While playing to win is sometimes associated with choosing a winning strategy, it is also incredibly relevant when it comes to connecting people around a culture of performance and mobilizing them to act passionately for maximum achievement.

Retired Rear Admiral Mark T. Guadagnini, former commander of Naval Air Training, told me about what it means to him to play to win. It begins with what he calls a "sense of mission accomplishment," which is "the ability to go out under any circumstances and to make sure the job gets done, gets done right, and gets done right every time." He went on to say: "It's about creating a sense of urgency—a feeling that you must win. [In the Navy], we don't train people not to lose. We train them to win. And that's the overwhelming feeling that is of primary importance when you're in combat because lives are at stake and our way of life is on the line.[29]

Even when the stakes are less momentous, playing to win— and creating that sense of mission accomplishment—can be the force used to deliver whatever goals an organization encompasses, from a nonprofit's social priority to improve lives, to the determination to be the best in any given industry. The salient point is that playing to win needs to align purpose and goals, and it needs to be a part of a sustainable cultural imperative. Life is Good, with its goal to "spread the power of optimism," for instance, can focus on winning in its own way, just as readily as Netflix, with its culture of freedom and responsibility, can do the same. There is no one-size-fits-all approach to creating the will to win, but there are building blocks that you can put into place.

Think Big

The first way to play to win is to create a compelling end goal. Jim Collins and Jerry Porras introduced the notion of a BHAG, or "Big Hairy Audacious Goal": a long-term ambition to mobilize the organization and stimulate progress. Here's what Collins and Porras say about it: "A BHAG engages people—it reaches out and grabs them in the gut. . . . It is tangible, energizing, and highly focused. . . . People 'get it' right away; it takes little or no explanation." Examples include these: "Every book, ever printed, in any language, all available in less than 60 seconds" (Amazon); Enable human exploration and settlement of Mars (paraphrasing SpaceX); and "A computer on every desk and in every home" (Microsoft).

Big River Steel's "think big" goal—to reinvent what it means to be a steel company—drove the steel start-up to make major waves right out of the gate. When it was founded in 2014, the Big River facility was the biggest economic development project in Arkansas history, the biggest construction project in the state, and one of the most technologically advanced. They were EBITDA positive in their second month of operation, the only steel production facility to be LEED certified for safety, and they were actively out scouting for "rebels who dare to go big" to join the company. All of those "think big" goals are helping them achieve their compelling vision of the future.

Thinking big, with a BHAG or another type of momentous goal, drives achievement under certain conditions.

First, the momentous goal *needs to be strategic*. It should guide business and product development and direct how an organization focuses its resources. Volvo's BHAG—"By 2020, no one should be killed or injured in a new Volvo car"—speaks volumes to the carmaker's designers, safety experts, and factory workers as they move into the age of driverless cars. Next, the "think big" objective *needs to push people to act*. The 2020 deadline in Volvo's BHAG creates and sustains the sense of urgency, just as Walmart's did in 1990 when the company pledged "to become a $125 billion company by year 2000." Last, the goal *needs to have an emotional appeal* to engage employees. Volvo's objective to eliminate driving deaths easily fits the bill, as does SpaceX's vision of enabling human exploration. Both are compelling enough to grab ahold of people and inspire them to act.

Thinking big and being able to articulate a specific and compelling vision for the future encourages and empowers people to act in service of achievement.

Be Best or Bust

The next play-to-win tactic is to aspire to be the best. This commitment to innovation and excellence helps fine-tune operational issues such as hiring and performance management, and it gives employees a strong sense of ownership and pride.

One way to be the best is to get there first. Big River Steel, for instance, was founded to be the world's first "Flex Mill," meaning it was set up to produce a wide range of product types for automotive, energy, construction, and agricultural industries. This "first" designation not only set the company apart instantly and gave it a reason to be in business, but it also helped form the company's thinking on several core issues. Innovation—Big River needed to be technologically advanced. Hiring—the company needed people who could be trained to use new equipment. Values—they were blazing new territory so they needed to set a high standard with their safety and sustainability scores.

If being first means writing the rules, then being the best means creating a center of excellence. This can be powerfully aspirational in terms of creating a plan for the future—wanting to be the best electronics retailer helped motivate Best Buy during their Renew Blue phase. Being first can also motivate an organization to continue innovating. For instance, Home Depot considered itself to be the best in class in big-box home improvement stores going way back. To hold on to that distinction, the company realized in 2007 that its information technology infrastructure required a dramatic upgrade. It was a major investment, and Home Depot made it happen to remain best in class. Today, technology connects their online and in-store business to give people a more seamless customer experience.

Both motivational and aspirational, being "best or bust" drives high achievement. It sends a signal to employees that they are standard bearers with a responsibility to make the most of the distinction. It is a bold option that is high risk and equally high reward for those that play to win.

Have a Way to Win

Last, playing to win requires not just a brilliant plan for proceeding but also a plan for winning. Former Rear Admiral Guadagnini, who flew over 90 combat missions for the Navy in five separate conflicts, told me about his plan for winning. Called the "Warrior Ethos," it includes the "sense of mission accomplishment" mentioned above as well three other elements.

The sense of mission accomplishment is important because it distills the impulse for urgency that winning in a complex, competitive situation requires, but that's just the beginning. The next element is called "disciplined aggression," which is the ability to operate within the parameters that you're given to aggressively accomplish the mission.

"The reason I say 'disciplined' is because the military is not an unlimited resource organization," Guadagnini said. "We have limitations on people and on equipment. There are parameters within which you must operate as well as the rules of engagement and international law."

This idea encompasses constantly taking action using the resources at hand and managing the limitations—and then forging toward the outcome that is desired.

The last two elements are "flexibility" and "bravery." In the military setting, flexibility is having the adaptability to draw on orders and training "and put them together in an adaptive manner so that they can accomplish the mission in the face of circumstances that may have advanced from the original plan." Bravery, in Guadagnini's model for winning in combat, is "the ability to act, think, and make decisions that will garner a successful outcome despite those physical and/or perceived things that would instill fear in a human being, and to overcome that fear to think, and to take actions that are required to accomplish the mission."

The Warrior Ethos comes down four adaptive elements that apply in the organizational context as well as in the military setting. Best Buy had its plan to Renew Blue. Netflix had its culture deck. Regardless of the particular points of your plan, having a way to win serves as yet another element to orient you toward achievement.

4. Foster Resilience

The last component of the killer achievement element of In Great Company is *resilience*—the ability to bounce back fast in the face of adversity and even failure. With resilience, the payback is derived by learning from painful experiences and being able to adapt and become better than ever. First introduced in the field of ecology to explain the adaptive capacity of an ecosystem, resilience is useful everywhere. For the purposes of the achievement, there are three important things to consider about this magic bullet ability.

First, *resilience improves our odds of success.* In her landmark research on motivation and mindset, noted psychologist Carol Dweck observed the differences between individuals who assumed their abilities were fixed and individuals who believed their abilities were fluid and subject to change and growth. Those with a growth mindset performed significantly better on difficult and challenging tasks.[30] And leaders agree with her findings. For instance, one survey of executives reported that 76 percent of people at the board level considered resilience to be a prerequisite for success. Yet, regardless of its perceived importance, only 10 percent of people at any level said that their organization placed a lot of emphasis on building and maintaining resilience.[31]

Next, *resilience is more important than ever.* Today, with technological advances and strategic shifts coming at us at a dizzying pace, and 69 percent of executives reporting that their organizations have experienced disruptive change,[32] the ability to adapt and proceed amidst increasing uncertainty is a crucial leadership trait at every level of organizations. According to Jim Citrin, "Adapting to change, taking in new information, and actually applying it in smart ways, is a core criteria of great CEOs right now."

Finally, *resilience can be learned.* Resilience is not a trait that we must be blessed with at birth. According to the American Psychological Association (APA), "resilience is not a trait that people either have or do not have. It involves behaviors, thoughts, and actions that can be learned and developed in anyone."[33] Dweck's work, as well, has shown that you can develop a growth mindset and increase your capacity for resilience in order to achieve goals and become better.

With achievement in mind, I coach leaders to focus on a few specific aspects of resilience in themselves and people working around them to foster this positive capability at the workplace level.

Focus on Strengths

Although we tend to associate resilience with overcoming weakness, a large part of the benefit comes from leveraging strengths.

As a path to emotional connectedness, focusing on strengths happens on multiple levels. The *individual level*: It's difficult to be achievement focused if you do not know your own strengths and weaknesses. Successful executives are actively self-reflective. They search themselves, openly ask for feedback, and adapt their behavior and decisions based on what they learn. The *leadership level*: Gallup has found that building employees' strengths is a far more effective approach to improving performance than trying to address weaknesses. When employees know and use their strengths, they are more engaged, perform better, and are less likely to leave the company.[34] The *team level*: Consider how much stronger a team will be when we understand each person's strengths and put teams together accordingly. With a strengths-based approach, collaboration is far more effective, and engagement is higher.[35]

For the purposes of resilience, it's critical to be able to call upon strengths to overcome the challenges we face along the path to achievement.

Fail Forward

Seen through the lens of resilience, failure uncovers viable opportunities for success. After all, we need to know what ideas, decisions, and behaviors fall flat in order to see what will work. Many of the most innovative organizations today seem to understand this, and they have policies in place that make failure acceptable as a stepping stone along the speculative path to success.

One of the tenets in the Netflix culture deck, for instance is, "You may have heard that preventing error is cheaper than fixing it. Yes, in manufacturing or medicine. Not so in creative environments." In other words, in an entrepreneurial organization, people fail forward by following a few simple steps. First, they make many small bets at once, thereby minimizing the impact of any one misstep and maximizing the chance of finding a success somewhere in the batch. Next, they create an environment of experimentation, whereby people make their best guess and try things to see what larger lesson can be learned. Last, they abide by the iterative process. When an idea hits a wall, you adjust the premise or pivot in order to proceed forward.

Even more than making failure acceptable, some organizations reward it. Intuit hosts "failure parties," P&G has its "Heroic Failure Award," and Grey Advertising has a trophy engraved to commemorate major project flops. And W.L. Gore? They celebrate failure with beer or champagne as a way to live into their fundamental belief: "Action is prized; ideas are encouraged; and making mistakes is viewed as part of the creative process."[36]

For resilient organizations, the one rule they all adhere to is embracing failure to leverage the learning. As Richard Branson has said, you don't learn to walk by following rules. "You learn by doing and by falling over."[37]

Manage Burnout

One high-achieving manufacturing executive I know was passionate about her job. She worked long hours and was promoted rapidly up the ranks and eventually into a C-suite position. She accepted awards and received one accolade after another. It seemed like nothing could stop her, until something did: burnout. First, she became run-down from all the traveling and long hours. Then she started feeling depressed and was having trouble sleeping. Finally, she decided to take time off, and she ultimately left the company altogether to run a social impact organization.

This tale of corporate misadventure is all too common. Studies have shown that the characteristics we associate with high achievement, such as perfectionism and other type A traits, are also associated with higher levels of burnout.[38] Related research has shown that 20 to 50 percent of employee turnover is due to burnout.[39]

This is a serious problem for leaders who want to set people up for success as part of an In Great Company workplace. As part of the fix, we need to balance a high-performance culture with supportive, empathetic practices that nurture the people who bring their all to the office every day.

For example, the consulting firm Point B was named *Fortune*'s number 1 "Best Medium Workplace" in the nation, in part because the company actively works at combating burnout in its employees. Point B makes travel optional, for example, employees dictate their own work schedules based on client needs, and if a consultant logs more than 60 hours in one week, managers step in to add a second consultant on the account.[40]

We can combat burnout with commonsense policies and fair work practices: making sure roles are clear, the workload is manageable, and people are not tackling low-value tasks that can easily be outsourced. In addition, burnout and other workload factors need to be addressed in solutions-focused performance conversations. More than anything, managers need to create a supportive work environment that fosters resilience. People should feel comfortable speaking up before they get sidelined by burnout.

Killer achievement is a core element of EC, and, along with the other four elements, it is a driver of being In Great Company. But it is also an outcome. When an organization is set up and structured for killer achievement, people are engaged in winning not only for themselves but also for the greater success of their colleagues and the organization.

KILLER ACHIEVEMENT: EXECUTIVE SUMMARY

Positive Best Practices	Ground Rules
Align strategy with structure.	Balance focus and flexibility. Communicate goals clearly. Set people free to achieve. Channel feedback for achievement.
Set people up to succeed.	Train continuously. Make learning inclusive.
Play to win.	Think big. Be best or bust. Have a way to win.
Foster resilience.	Focus on strengths. Fail forward. Manage burnout.

CHAPTER 8

CONCLUSION: FIVE THINGS TO DO RIGHT NOW

Being In Great Company is not something that concludes. As I have said, it is an ongoing endeavor in pursuit of personal high performance and organizational transformation. The more you contribute to this program personally, and together as an organization, the bigger the payback will be in the form of emotional connectedness, engagement, employee retention, and high achievement. And while the pursuit never ends, you must decide where to begin.

With that in mind, I have five steps directed at immediate action. They are based on my coaching agenda, and they will help you accelerate out the gate, organize around the ideas in this book, and plan to measure your progress along the path to success. You can lean into the first step, or you can jump ahead if you are already prepared, invested, and somewhere in the process of becoming In Great Company (Figure 8.1).

FIGURE 8.1

1. Discovery

I have coached you throughout this book on the paramount importance of self-awareness and discovering your strengths and development needs. To be In Great Company, you need to be clear with yourself and open with others on two overlapping dimensions: individually and organizationally.

Individually: Know where you stand along the path to becoming an emotionally connected leader. *The questions in Appendix A act as an ideal self-assessment tool.* Use them to determine your strengths and development needs. Ask your peers, direct reports, and fellow leaders to review the questions and provide you with 360-degree feedback. Include trusted outside stakeholders in the process. Customers, vendors, and other members of your value chain will be eager and able to help you become a better leader.

Organizationally: Determine the health of your company and how far you and your colleagues need to go (and in what areas) to be emotionally connected and In Great Company. *Use the Sample Employee Pulse Survey in Appendix B as a tool to take the temperature of the organization.* Assign project leaders in HR and across functions, and make sure that executives act as sponsors. Although the discovery step is only the beginning, leaders need to be the first and best champions of change.

2. Goal Setting

Use the results of your personal and organizational assessments to determine your needs. Go deeper by examining the vital statistics that define your organization. Compare annual data over a five-year period pertaining to employee and customer retention, loyalty scores, sales, and bottom-line results. Which way are they trending, and what story does that tell you?

Use this information to determine what you are solving for. What is central to your problem statement: Employee or customer attrition? Decreasing sales? Lack of innovation? Poor engagement scores? Underutilization of resources? Agree on the strengths that you will build on. Which elements of EC are you strongest in? Where do you stand on the crucial "respect" element?

Next, use the five dimensions of the In Great Company framework to set stretch goals that are achievable. Create one or two guiding objectives that connect back to the overall problems you are solving for. Create a small number of cascading goals that you can measure and manage over time. Ask yourself: "Do these goals address our core concerns? Are they meaningful to people across the organization? If we take the same pulse survey and self-assessments a year from now, will we be able to gauge our progress?"

Finally, create a communication strategy that will both inform and engage people to work together to achieve these goals in a way that brings people together in pursuit of becoming emotionally connected and In Great Company.

3. Coaching

The In Great Company approach is designed to bring people closer and give them the support they need to achieve great things. The most critical support mechanism for sparking emotional connectedness is coaching. As discussed, an emotionally connected leader is more coach than traditional manager.

Once goals are clear, coaching conversations can occur regularly with leader- and peer-coaches creating the backbone of support, guidance, and accountability. In fact, in some of the companies where I've worked to help create a coaching culture, everyone in the organization had access to coaching, whether the coach was a peer, manager, or professional executive coach. Everyone received the support and guidance they needed. Regardless of the coaching lineup, trust and confidentiality are the two main ingredients of the relationship. The coach must be respectful, collaborative, and clear on goals. The people being coached need to be respectful, open, and eager to be active participants in their development journey.

MAKE COACHING A CORE CAPABILITY

The material in this box is based on and adapted from Marshall Goldsmith and Sal Silvester's "Stakeholder Centered Coaching Model."[1]

Coach Responsibilities

► Tailor the process to the leader's needs and schedule.

► Assist the leader in crafting goals and enlisting stakeholders.

► Accommodate leader's schedule for calls and meetings.

► Provide honest assessment, healthy challenge, and strong support.

► Recap conversations and return calls and e-mails in a timely manner.

► Provide support to stakeholders, and ensure that the process is working.

► Model strong skills for giving and receiving feedback and suggestions.

► Honor highest level of trust and confidentiality.

Leader Responsibilities

► Identify and reflect on your core values.

► Commit to goal, and share it with stakeholders.

► Enlist stakeholders for challenge and support (humility).

► Try behaviors that are outside your comfort zone (courage).

► Follow up with stakeholders.

► Debrief regularly with the coach.

► Focus on the "end in mind." *(continues)*

Both

- ▶ Engage with respect.
- ▶ Collaborate to achieve goals.
- ▶ Celebrate success.

4. Measurement

At the leadership level, measurement is where you prove you are a steward of change. One of the tools I use for measurement consists of a dashboard to mark progress along the five elements of EC. (See Figure 8.2.)

I also repeat the self-assessments and pulse surveys to gauge granular progress over time. Regardless of what specific format you use, measurement needs to happen regularly with a methodology that is fair, inclusive, and informed by data. Other informal measurement tools that lend themselves to this coaching-based approach are brief, concise check-ins with stakeholders, occasional after-action reviews, and an annual full-cycle debriefing of learnings, milestones, and missteps. For me, measurement is an opportunity to reinforce the In Great Company dynamic whereby we all succeed together—no blame—and our next steps are based on what we have learned.

5. Practice

This is the place where change really occurs—through ongoing, everyday practice. With the In Great Company approach, each of us is equally responsible for sparking emotional connectedness and

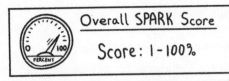

Area	Your Area Score	Statement	Your Statement Score
Systemic Collaboration		Teamwork and collaboration among associates are valued in my company.	___%
		People in my company give me advice for what I can do better in the future.	___%
		In the past two weeks, I have been a part of a team focused on a specific project.	___%
Positive Future		People in my company are open to new ideas.	___%
		People in my company demonstrate a positive attitude toward the future.	___%
Alignment of Values		My company lives the values it promotes.	___%
		My company stands for honesty and integrity.	___%
		Associates in my company are held accountable for their actions.	___%
Respect		My ideas and contributions are respected in my company.	___%
		In the past two weeks, someone in my company has made me feel that my work is appreciated.	___%
		My manager trusts me.	___%
Killer Achievement		My coworkers are competent and knowledgeable.	___%
		Effort and hard work are valued in my company.	___%
		We as associates work toward shared goals in my company.	___%

FIGURE 8.2 *Overall SPARK Score (Percentage)*

creating a workplace where people are committed to getting better each day, not only for ourselves but for our colleagues and customers.

As so much of the advice in this book demonstrates, the way to engage a broad group of people is to keep the commitment simple and actionable. As part of that, I use "clear active questions" to empower people and remind them that their actions make a difference. These are questions that people should ask themselves as they continue to work the In Great Company approach:

Systemic Collaboration

- ▶ Do I value teamwork and collaboration?
- ▶ Do I openly give and accept advice for being better in the future?
- ▶ In the past two weeks, have I been part of a team or collaborated to solve a problem?

Positive Future

- ▶ Am I open to new ideas?
- ▶ In the last two weeks, have I demonstrated a positive outlook for the future?

Alignment of Values

- ▶ Are my values and the organization's values in sync?
- ▶ Do I stand for honesty and integrity?
- ▶ Do I hold myself and others accountable for practicing our values?

Respect

- ▶ Do I show respect for the people I work with and expect the same from my colleagues?
- ▶ In the past two weeks, have I expressed gratitude or appreciation for someone else's work, effort, or accomplishments?

Killer Achievement

- ▶ Am I known to be competent and knowledgeable?
- ▶ Do I support others and help them succeed?
- ▶ Do I work toward the shared goals in my company?

These simple questions illustrate why the In Great Company model sparks emotional connectedness—because when we show that we care about our colleagues and support their efforts to succeed and achieve, then the same benefits accrue to us.

I have seen it happen in numerous organizations: The automaker with deteriorating productivity numbers. The private insurance firm that had an endemic problem with ethics. The tech start-up that was losing people faster than the company could onboard and train new recruits. Each of these organizations and others turned the tide by providing people with a process where they could work together to achieve something meaningful—a workplace that is better for everyone. When everyone benefits, everyone gets engaged, and vice versa: when everyone is engaged, everyone benefits.

I invite you to get engaged, emotionally connected, and In Great Company beginning today. *The In Great Company Best Practices Playbook in Appendix C offers dozens of ways to actively change things for the better.* Working with others to create a workplace that you love is more than engaging. It's contagious.

LEADER'S SELF-ASSESSMENT: DO I LEAD IN GREAT COMPANY?

Take this self-assessment to determine your strengths and areas of weakness as a leader. Use what you learn to put together a development plan for yourself.

Systemic Collaboration

1. Do you monitor for equal airtime in conversations?
2. Do you ensure that four roles are equally played when leading a team conversation (that is, challenger, supporter, mirror, and mover)?
3. How present are you during conversations?
4. Do you engage in difficult conversations with empathy?
5. Do you consider the opinions and thinking of your stakeholders and supporters?

Positive Future

6. What is your purpose and passion in your work?

7. What is your purpose and passion in your life? Is there overlap?

8. Do you believe you are living your work and life passions and purpose?

9. Have you ever channeled your passion into products or sales?

10. Do you actively recruit or seek out people with passion for your work?

11. Do you learn from people who are performing at high levels?

12. Do you give your highest performers opportunities to teach others about their successes?

13. Are your communications for your vision for the future clear, purposeful, and meaningful to others?

14. How often do you reinforce this message?

15. Do you give advice for people to get better at specific behaviors or tasks, or do you focus only on what they have done incorrectly?

Alignment of Values

16. Do you hold others accountable for their actions—and keep it in line with company values?

17. Do you hold yourself responsible for your work?

18. Are you successful in making a business case for others around the values of the company?

19. Do you tie performance to values?

20. How well do you create a business case for measuring values as a means to achieving business strategy?

21. Do you ensure that the way people achieve is in alignment with the company values?

22. Do you have partners to help keep you accountable for your goals and values?

Respect

23. Do you ensure that respect is reciprocal in your communication?
24. What kinds of data sources do you use to make sure you understand your customers' needs?
25. Do you conduct yourself in a civil manner?
26. How do you regulate your emotions in times of conflict?
27. In what ways do you show empathy to others during times when they are in need of help?
28. Do you make inclusion a part of your business strategy?
29. To what degree do you believe you are self-aware?
30. To what degree do you believe others think you are self-aware?
31. For what do you feel most grateful at work?
32. For what do you feel most grateful in life?

Killer Achievement

33. To what degree do you balance focus on goals with flexibility?
34. Do you communicate your goals clearly and consistently to others?
35. Do you give yourself or others the resources, help, and support they may need to achieve collective goals?
36. Is being best in class important to you?
37. Do you consider succeeding in your goal (that is, winning) an integral part of your process?
38. Do you train and develop only at certain times, or do you train and develop yourself and others continuously?
39. Do you focus on developing strengths?
40. Is failure understood to be a part of the learning process?
41. How do you ensure recovery or avoidance of burnout?

APPENDIX B

SAMPLE EMPLOYEE PULSE SURVEY: ARE YOUR ASSOCIATES IN GREAT COMPANY?

P lease indicate your level of agreement with the following statements: strongly disagree, disagree, somewhat disagree, somewhat agree, agree, strongly agree:

1. Teamwork and collaboration among associates are valued in my company.
2. People in my company give me advice for what I can do better in the future.
3. In the past two weeks, I have been part of a team focused on a specific project.
4. People in my company are open to new ideas.

5. In the last two weeks, people in my company have demonstrated a positive attitude toward the future.

6. My coworkers are competent and knowledgeable.

7. Effort and hard work are valued in my company.

8. We as associates work toward shared goals in my company.

9. My company lives the values it promotes.

10. My company stands for honesty and integrity.

11. Associates in my company are held accountable for their actions.

12. My ideas and contributions are respected in my company

13. In the past two weeks, someone in my company has made me feel that my work is appreciated.

14. My manager trusts me.

15. I would recommend working at this company to a friend or business colleague.

THE IN GREAT COMPANY BEST PRACTICES PLAYBOOK

U se this focused advice to make the shifts you need to become In Great Company.

SYSTEMIC COLLABORATION

Positive Best Practices	Ground Rules
Equal airtime	Make equal airtime a management priority. Address the collaboration killers. Use an icebreaker. Ensure a balance of team roles. Maintain focus.
Mindful listening	Be fully present. Take a listening tour. Defer judgment. Engage with empathy.　*(continues)*

Positive Best Practices	Ground Rules
Free flow of information	Incentivize information sharing. Work across functions. Focus on the magic middle. Extend the openness to the outside.
Mix of structure and flexibility	Combine freedom and focus. Use the power of people. Build accountability into collaboration.
Conflict resolution	Don't skip steps. Neutralize the negative. Get beyond consensus.

POSITIVE FUTURE

Positive Best Practices	Ground Rules
Leverage passion.	Let purpose drive passion. Turn passion into products. Let passion pivot. Look for passionate persuaders. Put passion in its place.
Turn change into a positive.	Neutralize the pain of change. Get positive with "deviants." Offer more ways to change.
Create space to innovate.	Stay future focused. Put risk in perspective. Make innovation for everyone. Be ambidextrous.
Keep workplace practices positive.	Create a climate of optimism. Feedforward. Start with *yes, and*.

ALIGNMENT OF VALUES

Positive Best Practices	Ground Rules
Make values meaningful and memorable.	Get existential. Be aspirational. Cocreate core values. Think broadly about audience.
Practice what you promote.	Overcommunicate your values. Live by the values you promote. Act with empathy and compassion. Lead by example.
Self-select and self-correct.	Prepare candidates to self-select. Screen for values. Ask about specific situations. Consider the level or function of an employee.
Remember to measure.	Keep top management accountable. Create the business case. Remember to track the how. Use partners to keep you accountable.

RESPECT

Positive Best Practices	Ground Rules
Make respect mutual.	Pass the trust test. Create a culture of civility. Put fairness first.
Respect differences.	Dig deeper with data. View inclusion broadly. Make inclusion mission critical.
Lead with respect.	Practice self-awareness. Communicate your respect.
The small things are big.	Go heavy on gratitude. Consider the human experience.

KILLER ACHIEVEMENT

Positive Best Practices	Ground Rules
Align strategy with structure.	Balance focus and flexibility. Communicate goals clearly. Set people free to achieve. Channel feedback for achievement.
Set people up to succeed.	Train continuously. Make learning inclusive.
Play to win.	Think big. Be best or bust. Have a way to win.
Foster resilience.	Focus on strengths. Fail forward. Manage burnout.

RESEARCH METHODOLOGY

The purpose of the research effort surrounding this book was to test how loving one's workplace affected employee and organizational outcomes, and what elements or conditions led people to love their workplace.

Study 1

We tested the psychometric properties of a scale measuring feelings of love toward one's workplace, in part to determine the elements people most wanted to find there. The participants were 473 individuals (212 women, 261 men; average age 33) sourced from Amazon's Mechanical Turk (MTurk).

All participants worked at least 20 hours a week at a job outside of Mechanical Turk. They responded to a series of questions designed to measure feelings of love toward one's workplace. They were also interviewed regarding the aspects of an organization that made them feel most valued.

Themes emerged from these interviews, with the most positively cited themes being: teamwork, honesty and integrity, appreciation and support, emphasis on looking forward, and focus on achievement (see Table D.1).

TABLE D.1 THEMES THAT EMERGED FROM INTERVIEWS

Theme	Components	Definition
Teamwork	Teamwork, collaboration, communication	Employees value teamwork and collaboration along with open communication channels where information and feedback are shared freely.
Honest and integrity	Ethics, work ethic, values, accountability, reliability, ownership, transparency	Employees want to work in a workplace that places an emphasis on honesty, integrity, and ethics. They want employees and leaders that are reliable and held accountable for their actions.
Appreciation and support	Appreciation and recognition, respect, trust, listening, compassion, empathy, fairness, support	Employees want to be appreciated and recognized for achievements. They want to work in an environment where they feel respected, trusted, and listened to—a workplace that is fair and supportive.

Theme	Components	Definition
Forward looking	Positivity, innovation, openness, passion, pride	Employees want to work in a positive environment that fosters innovation and openness.
Achievement	Effort, commitment, focus on customer, competence, work processes, learning, shared goals, professionalism	Employees want to work in a workplace where effort and hard work are valued, a workplace where processes are in place, and where they can focus on the customer and work toward shared goals.

From this framework, three to five concepts were developed for each theme. These statements were then tested for reliability and validity. Participants completed the survey along with demographic information. Items for inclusion in the final measure were selected using a standard statistical research methodology.

Study 2

We tested loving one's workplace as an independent construct and measured its relationship with important employee outcomes in comparison to organizational commitment, in order to determine its utility and the construct validity of the assessment.

The participants were 214 individuals (97 women, 117 men; average age 39) sourced from MTurk, all of whom worked at least 20 hours a week at an outside job. They completed a survey to test the following hypotheses:

▶ *Hypothesis 1:* Loving one's work will positively correlate with organizational citizenship behaviors.

▶ *Hypothesis 2:* Loving one's work will account for variance in organizational citizenship behaviors beyond that of affective commitment.

▶ *Hypothesis 3:* Loving one's work will positively correlate with psychological safety.

▶ *Hypothesis 4:* Loving one's work will account for variance in psychological safety beyond that of affective commitment.

▶ *Hypothesis 5:* Loving one's work will positively correlate with self-reported performance.

▶ *Hypothesis 6:* Loving one's work will account for variance in self-reported performance beyond that of affective commitment.

Results showed that hypotheses 1, 3, 4, 5, and 6 were statistically supported and hypothesis 2 was not statistically supported.

Study 3

The study surveyed 300 participants (130 women, 170 men; average age 38) to determine the relationship between one's score on the 14-item Most Loved Workplaces (MLWs) scale and self-reported personality traits, including these:

▶ Agreeableness
▶ Conscientiousness
▶ Neuroticism
▶ Openness to new experiences

The results indicated that there was a relationship between individual employees' dispositions and how they felt about their work. For instance, conscientious employees were more likely to love their work, while employees who were highly neurotic were less likely to love their work.

Study 4

The study surveyed 2,642 employees from one Fortune 1000 organization to test their overall Most Loved Workplace (MLW) score and to determine how it was likely to affect organizational performance and outcomes. Employees were in North America, Europe, the Middle East, and Africa. The largest group of respondents were 30 years or younger, but all age groups were represented. Within the respondent group, 65 percent were male, and about 70 percent of the sample had been with the organization between one and five years.

Sample findings attributed to this organization are the following:

▶ Overall mean index score was 76 percent (out of a possible 100 percent, with a high score indicating positive feelings).

▶ Employees who were with the company less than one year had significantly higher means than all other groups, and employees who were with the company one to two years had significantly higher means than those who were with the company three to four years.

▶ No significant differences were found between various age groups, male and female employees, across job types or regions. Employees in manufacturing, HR, and supply chains indicated a significantly lower level of workplace love than did employees in some of the other job functions.

▶ The high-scoring group had many more employees from sales than would be expected.

▶ The employees in Europe had many fewer employees represented in the high-scoring group than would be expected and more in both the low- and medium-scoring groups.

Other

The above findings supplement the author's over 20 years of collecting and synthesizing learnings from dialogue groups and peer coaching C-level executives in hundreds of Fortune 1000 organizations.

Key Summary

The studies helped us determine what causes employees to love their organization, and what employers can do to cultivate that love in their company. The data showed where employees diverge between "most loved," "neutral," and "disliked" workplaces, and how those differences affect the bottom line on a daily basis.

Across every demographic, the desire to be respected drives the most loved workplace response. In most loved workplaces, 94 percent of employees have reported that they would likely work harder for their employer, with 59 percent reporting that they would be four times more likely to work harder and produce results.

Another response points to retention, with 95 percent of employees citing the positive feelings they have for their team, peers, subordinates, and bosses as the most relevant factor in their decision to stay with a company.

NOTES

Introduction

1. David G. Allen, Phillip C. Bryant, and James M. Vardaman, "Retaining Talent: Replacing Misconceptions with Evidence-Based Strategies," *Academy of Management Perspectives*, vol. 24, no. 2, 2010, pp. 48–64, http://www.jstor.org/stable /25682398.
2. *Wall Street Journal*, "How to Reduce Employee Turnover," *Wall Street Journal Guides*, April 7, 2009, http://guides.wsj.com/management/recruiting-hiring -and-firing/how-to-reduce-employee-turnover/tab/print/.
3. David Brown, Veronica Melian, Marc Solow, Sonny Chheng, and Kathy Parker, "Culture and Engagement: The Naked Organization," *Deloitte Insights*, February 27, 2015, https://www2.deloitte.com/insights/us/en/focus/human-capital -trends/2015/employee-engagement-culture-human-capital-trends-2015.html.
4. https://www.gallup.com/workplace/229424/employee-engagement.aspx. Accessed August 6, 2018.
5. See below and also Appendix D, "Research Methodology," for more on the research that underlies the model.
6. London School of Economics and Political Science, "When Performance-Related Pay Backfires," April 24, 2016, http://www.lse.ac.uk/website-archive/newsAnd Media/news/archives/2009/06/performancepay.aspx.
7. From my own research. See Appendix D, "Research Methodology."
8. Quoted from an e-mail exchange between Bob Maresca and the author, November 14, 2017.

Chapter 1

1. A. H. Maslow, "A Theory of Human Motivation," *Psychological Review*, vol. 50, no. 4, 1943, pp. 370–396; and A. H. Maslow, *Motivation and Personality*, Harper & Row, New York, 1954.
2. Debra Umberson and Jennifer Karas Montez, "Social Relationships and Health: A Flashpoint for Health Policy," *Journal of Health and Social Behavior*, vol. 51, no. 1, March 1, 2010, pp. S54–S66, http://journals.sagepub.com/doi/abs/10.11 77/0022146510383501?url_ver=Z39.88-2003&rfr_id=ori:rid:crossref.org&rfr _dat=cr_pub%3dpubmed.
3. Nicole K. Valtorta, Mona Kanaan, Simon Gilbody, Sara Ronzi, and Barbara Hanratty, "Loneliness and Social Isolation as Risk Factors for Coronary Heart Disease and Stroke: Systematic Review and Meta-analysis of Longitudinal

Observational Studies," *Heart*, vol. 102, no. 13, April 18, 2016, pp. 1009–1016, https://heart.bmj.com/content/102/13/1009.

4. Emma Seppälä, *The Happiness Track: How to Apply the Science of Happiness to Accelerate Your Success*, HarperOne, San Francisco, 2016.

5. Jane E. Brody, "Social Interaction Is Critical for Mental and Physical Health," *New York Times*, June 12, 2017, https://www.nytimes.com/2017/06/12/well/live /having-friends-is-good-for-you.html; and Emma Seppälä, "Connect to Thrive: Social Connection Improves Health, Well-Being & Longevity," *Psychology Today*, August 26, 2012, https://www.psychologytoday.com/us/blog/feeling-it/201208 /connect-thrive.

6. Virgin Pulse, "The Business of Healthy Employees: A Survey of Workplace Health Priorities," *Pulse Papers*, 2014, https://www.shrm.org/ResourcesAndTools/hr -topics/benefits/Documents/PulsePaper_BusinessHealthyEmployees2014.pdf.

7. John D. Mayer, Peter Salovey, and David R. Caruso, "Emotional Intelligence: New Ability or Eclectic Traits?" *American Psychologist*, vol. 63, no. 6, September 2008, pp. 503–517.

8. Daniel Goleman, *Emotional Intelligence*, Bantam Books, New York, 1995.

9. Christopher A. Bartlett, "GE's Two-Decade Transformation: Jack Welch's Leadership," *Harvard Business Review*, April 28, 1999, https://hbr.org/product/geo -s-two-decade-transformation-jack-welch-s-leader/an/399150-PDF-ENG.

10. Travis Bradberry, "How Successful People Stay Calm," *TalentSmart*, last modified 2018, http://www.talentsmart.com/articles/How-Successful-People-Stay-Calm -799773507-p-1.html.

11. Julia Rozovsky, "The Five Keys to a Successful Google Team," *re:Work*, November 17, 2015, https://rework.withgoogle.com/blog/five-keys-to-a-successful-google -team/.

12. Heidi K. Gardner and Herminia Ibarra, "How to Capture Value from Collaboration, Especially If You're Skeptical About It," *Harvard Business Review*, May 2, 2017, https://hbr.org/2017/05/how-to-capture-value-from-collaboration-especially -if-youre-skeptical-about-it.

13. Amy Edmondson, "Psychological Safety and Learning Behavior in Work Teams," *Administrative Science Quarterly*, vol. 44, no. 2, June 1999, pp. 350–383, doi:10.2307/2666999.

14. Natalie J. Allen and John P. Meyer, "The Measurement and Antecedents of Affective, Continuance, and Normative Commitment to the Organization," *Journal of Occupational Psychology*, vol. 53, 1990, pp. 337–338.

15. Linda Rhoades, Robert Eisenberger, and Stephen Armeli, "Affective Commitment to the Organization: The Contribution of Perceived Organizational Support," *Journal of Applied Psychology*, vol. 86, no. 5, 2001, pp. 825–836, http://dx.doi .org/10.1037/0021-9010.86.5.825.

16. Francesca Gino, "How to Make Employees Feel Like They Own Their Work," Harvard Business Review, December 7, 2015, https://hbr.org/2015/12/how-to -make-employees-feel-like-they-own-their-work.

17. Susan Weinschenk, "When People Feel Connected, They Work Harder," *Psychology Today*, April 22, 2016, https://www.psychologytoday.com/us/blog/brain-wise/201604/when-people-feel-connected-they-work-harder.

18. This quip is commonly attributed to Peter Drucker, but there's no published record to show that these are his words.

19. SHRM Foundation, "Engaging Your Employees," https://www.shrm.org/foundation/ourwork/initiatives/resources-from-past-initiatives/pages/engaging-your-employees.aspx; and Gallup, "Engage Your Employees to See High Performance and Innovation," https://www.gallup.com/workplace/229424/employee-engagement.aspx. Accessed August 15, 2018.

Chapter 2

1. John P. Kotter, "Leading Change: Why Transformation Efforts Fail," *Harvard Business Review*, May 1995, https://hbr.org/1995/05/leading-change-why-transformation-efforts-fail-2.

2. Tim Cook, *Apple CEO Tim Cook on Collaboration*, Fuqua School of Business, Duke University, video, 2:31 minutes, May 30, 2013, https://www.youtube.com/watch?v=EZPYLZ7I6gs.

3. Sam Palmisano and Errol Morris, *IBM THINK, IBM CEO Sam Palmisano with Errol Morris on Collaborative Leadership*, video, 1:23 minutes, September 20, 2011, https://www.youtube.com/watch?v=TAmBiPzVpf4.

4. Elisa Steele, *Enterprise Social Collaboration with Elisa Steele, CEO, Jive Software*, Conversations with Top Innovators, episode 143, video, 46:35 minutes, November 13, 2015, https://www.cxotalk.com/episode/enterprise-social-collaboration-elisa-steele-ceo-jive-software#transcript.

5. The Stairway to Collaboration figure and practice are inspired by a coaching model that Deborah Slobodnik taught me that is based on the Four-Player Model—the core concept of David Kantor's theory of structural dynamics published here: David Kantor, *Reading the Room: Group Dynamics for Coaches and Leaders*, Jossey-Bass/Wiley, San Francisco, 2012.

6. Elizabeth Weise, "Amazon's Jeff Bezos Urges Employees to 'Disagree and Commit,'" *USA TODAY*, April 13, 2017, https://www.usatoday.com/story/tech/news/2017/04/13/jeff-bezos-amazon-annual-shareholder-letter-day-1/100418722/.

7. "Top CEOs 2018: Employees' Choice," *Glassdoor*, May 2018, https://www.glassdoor.com/Award/Top-CEOs-LST_KQ0,8.htm.

8. Adam Lashinsky, "How CEO Marc Benioff Drives Relentless Forward Thinking at Salesforce," *Fortune*, October 19, 2017, http://fortune.com/2017/10/19/salesforce-marc-benioff-leadership/.

9. Carmine Gallo, "New Grads Should Follow PepsiCo CEO Indra Nooyi's 5-Step Success Model," *Forbes*, April 29, 2018, https://www.forbes.com/sites/carminegallo/2018/04/29/new-grads-should-follow-pepsico-ceo-indra-nooyis-5-step-success-model/#7f8c6f452038.

10. Nicole Skibola, "Leadership Lessons from WD-40's CEO, Garry Ridge," *Forbes*, June 27, 2011, https://www.forbes.com/sites/csr/2011/06/27/leadership-lessons -from-wd-40s-ceo-garry-ridge/#669926221fae.

11. Emmie Martin, "A Major Airline Says There's Something It Values More Than Its Customers, and There's a Good Reason Why," *Business Insider*, July 29, 2015, https://www.businessinsider.com/southwest-airlines-puts-employees-first-2015-7.

12. Barry Wehmiller, "Bob Chapman: Chairman & CEO," barrywehmiller network, https://www.barrywehmiller.com/our-business/leadership-team/bob-chapman. Accessed August 15, 2018.

13. Bob Chapman, "Why Your Company Should Measure Hearts, Not Heads," *LinkedIn*, October 25, 2016, https://www.linkedin.com/pulse/why-your-company-should -measure-hearts-heads-bob-chapman/.

14. Scott Leibs, "Putting People Before the Bottom Line (and Still Making Money)," *Inc.*, May 2014, https://www.inc.com/audacious-companies/scott-leibs/barry -wehmiller.html.

15. Giam Swiegers and Karen Toohey, "Waiter, Is That Inclusion in My Soup? A New Recipe to Improve Business Performance," Deloitte, 2013, https://www2.deloitte .com/content/dam/Deloitte/au/Documents/human-capital/deloitte-au-hc -diversity-inclusion-soup-0513.pdf.

16. Shula Nueman, "Too Much Trust Could Actually Be Bad for Business, Study Finds," *The Source*, Washington University in St. Louis, November 3, 2005, https://source.wustl.edu/2005/11/too-much-trust-could-actually-be-bad-for -business-study-finds/.

17. Jessica Amortegui, "Why Finding Meaning at Work Is More Important Than Feeling Happy," *Fast Company*, June 26, 2014, https://www.fastcompany.com /3032126/how-to-find-meaning-during-your-pursuit-of-happiness-at-work.

18. Monica Wang, "America's Favorite CEOs in 2016, and Why Their Employees Love Them," *Forbes*, June 10, 2016, https://www.forbes.com/sites /monicawang/2016/06/10/americas-favorite-ceos-in-2016-and-why-their -employees-love-them/#643165b91754.

19. Strengths-based leadership was popularized by Gallup in their book by Tom Rath and Barry Conchie, *Strength Based Leadership: Great Leaders, Teams, and Why People Follow*, Gallup Press, New York, 2008.

Chapter 3

1. Peter Jacobs, Bart Schlatmann, and Deepak Mahadevan, "ING's Agile Transformation," *McKinsey Quarterly*, January 2017, https://www.mckinsey.com/industries /financial-services/our-insights/ings-agile-transformation.

2. ING, "The ING Way of Working," ING., https://www.ing.jobs/Netherlands /Why-ING/What-we-offer/Agile-working.htm.

3. Eric Ries, *The Startup Way*, Crown, New York, 2017.

4. Brian Power, "How GE Applies Lean Startup Practices," *Harvard Business Review*, April 23, 2014, https://hbr.org/2014/04/how-ge-applies-lean-startup-practices.

5. Eric Ries, *The Lean Startup: How Today's Entrepreneurs Use Continuous Innovation to Create Radically Successful Businesses*, Crown, New York, 2011.

6. Cate Gutowski, "GE Digital Transformation: Collaboration Leads to Innovation," *CIO*, https://www.cio.com/article/3235344/digital-transformation/ge-digital-transformation-collaboration-leads-to-innovation.html.

7. Jodi Bradley, Teresa Lai, Sharon Meaney, Shannon Nguyen, and Karen Brady, "Cisco Collaboration Work Practice Study," *Cisco Public*, March 2013, https://www.cisco.com/c/dam/en/us/solutions/collaboration/collaboration-sales/cwps_full_report.pdf.

8. Priyanka B. Carr and Gregory M. Walton, "Cues of Working Together Fuel Intrinsic Motivation," *Journal of Experimental Social Psychology*, vol. 53, 2014, pp. 169–184, https://doi.org/10.1016/j.jesp.2014.03.015.

9. Erik Samdahl, "Top Employers Are 5.5x More Likely to Reward Collaboration," i4cp Productivity Blog, June 22, 2017, https://www.i4cp.com/productivity-blog/top-employers-are-5-5x-more-likely-to-reward-collaboration.

10. Adam Smiley Poswolsky, "What Millennial Employees Really Want," *Fast Company*, June 4, 2015, https://www.fastcompany.com/3046989/what-millennial-employees-really-want.

11. Tiffany McDowell, Dimple Agarwal, Don Miller, Tsutomu Okamoto, and Trevor Page, "Organizational Design: The Rise of Teams," *Deloitte Global Human Capital Trends*, 2016, https://www2.deloitte.com/insights/us/en/focus/human-capital-trends/2016/organizational-models-network-of-teams.html; and Ken Makovsky, "Dunbar's Number: A Key to Networking," *Forbes*, August 7, 2014, https://www.forbes.com/sites/kenmakovsky/2014/08/07/dunbars-number-and-the-need-for-relationship-management/#7388fe7a397b.

12. Lowell L. Bryan, Eric Matson, and Leigh M. Weiss, "Harnessing the Power of Informal Employee Networks," *McKinsey Quarterly*, November 2007, https://www.mckinsey.com/business-functions/organization/our-insights/harnessing-the-power-of-informal-employee-networks.

13. Ron Friedman, "The Collaboration Paradox: Why Working Together Often Yields Weaker Results," *99U*, https://99u.adobe.com/articles/27941/the-collaboration-paradox-why-working-together-often-yields-weaker-results.

14. Julia Rozovsky, "The Five Keys to a Successful Google Team," *re:Work*, November 17, 2015, https://rework.withgoogle.com/blog/five-keys-to-a-successful-google-team/.

15. Amy Edmondson, "Psychological Safety and Learning Behavior in Work Teams," *Administrative Science Quarterly*, vol. 44, no. 2, 1999, pp. 350–383, doi:10.2307/2666999.

16. Unless otherwise noted, in this chapter all quotes and paraphrased comments from Deborah Lipman Slobodnik are from my interview with Slobodnik on November 16, 2017.

17. Unless otherwise noted, in this chapter all quotes and paraphrased comments from Tom Kolditz are from my interview with Kolditz on March 28, 2018.

18. Ariel Bogle, "Atlassian's CEO on Why He Doesn't Watch His Company's Share Price," *Mashable*, May 31, 2016, https://mashable.com/2016/05/31/michael -cannon-brookes-atlassian/#wwJ.mmQipmqE.

19. Juliet Eilperin, "White House Women Want to Be in the Room Where It Happens," *Washington Post*, September 13, 2016, https://www.washingtonpost.com /news/powerpost/wp/2016/09/13/white-house-women-are-now-in-the-room -where-it-happens/?utm_term=.9ea97a06c035.

20. Sarah Greesonbach and Helen Russell, "How We Culture with Helen Russell, Chief People Officer at Atlassian," *Culture Summit*, March 26, 2018, https:// www.culturesummit.co/articles/how-we-culture-helen-russell-atlassian/.

21. Unless otherwise noted, in this chapter quotes from Brian Fishel are from my interview with Brian Fishel on February19, 2018.

22. Guy Itzchakov, Kenneth G. DeMarree, Avraham N. Kluger, and Yaara Turjeman-Levi, "The Listener Sets the Tone: High-Quality Listening Increases Attitude Clarity and Behavior-Intention Consequences," *Personality and Social Psychology Bulletin*, vol. 44, no. 5, 2018, pp. 762–778, http://journals.sagepub.com/doi/abs /10.1177/0146167217747874?journalCode=pspc.

23. Guy Itzchakov and Avraham N. Kluger, "The Power of Listening in Helping People Change," *Harvard Business Review*, May 17, 2018, https://hbr.org/2018/05/the -power-of-listening-in-helping-people-change.

24. Ibid.

25. Annie Pillon, "UPS CEO Explains Why Listening Is So Important to Leaders," *Small Business Trends*, June 9, 2017, https://smallbiztrends.com/2017/06/why-leaders -should-listen.html.

26. Atlassian, "Company Values," last modified 2018, https://www.atlassian.com /company/values.

27. Mike Cannon-Brookes, "Let's Open up Work, Together," Atlassian blog, September 13, 2017, https://www.atlassian.com/blog/announcements/lets-open-up-work-together.

28. Pamela Newenham, "Five Ways to Create a Culture of Innovation in the Workplace," *Irish Times* (Dublin, Ireland), October 14, 2013, https://www.irishtimes .com/business/five-ways-to-create-a-culture-of-innovation-in-the-workplace -1.1557801.

29. Atlassian, "Atlassian Announces Fourth Quarter and Fiscal Year 2017 Results," *Atlassian Investor Relations*, July 27, 2017, https://investors.atlassian.com/investors -overview/default.aspx.

30. Atlassian, "Leadership Team Health Monitor," *Atlassian: Team Playbook*, last modified 2018, https://www.atlassian.com/team-playbook/health-monitor/leadership -teams; and Sophie Wade, "Unlearning to Live with Change: How to Hire, Respond and Succeed in an Evolving Environment," *HuffPost*, August 11, 2017, https://www.huffingtonpost.com/entry/unlearning-to-live-with-change-how-to -hire-respond_us_598dca13e4b063e2ae057f0b.

31. Michael Arena, Rob Cross, Jonathan Sims, and Mary Uhl-Bien, "How to Catalyze Innovation in Your Organization," *MIT Sloan Management Review*, June 13,

2017, https://sloanreview.mit.edu/article/how-to-catalyze-innovation-in-your
-organization/?article=how-to-catalyze-innovation-in-your-organization&post
_type=article.

32. Unless otherwise noted, in this chapter any quotes and paraphrased comments from Michael Arena that are not otherwise attributed are from my interview with Arena on February 4, 2018.

33. Daniel Roberts, "At W.L. Gore, 57 Years of Authentic Culture," *Fortune*, March 5, 2015, http://fortune.com/2015/03/05/w-l-gore-culture/.

34. Rob Cross, Reb Rebele, and Adam Grant, "Collaborative Overload," *Harvard Business Review*, January-February 2016, https://hbr.org/2016/01/collaborative -overload.

35. Rob Cross, Wayne Baker, and Andrew Parker, "What Creates Energy in Organizations," *MIT Sloan Management Review*, July 15, 2003, https://sloanreview.mit .edu/article/what-creates-energy-in-organizations/.

36. Unless otherwise noted, in this chapter all quotes and paraphrased comments from George Mitchell are from my interview with Mitchell on October 21, 2009, at the Linkage Global Institute for Leadership Development.

37. Christopher Voss, interview with the author on February 21, 2018.

Chapter 4

1. Unless otherwise noted, in this chapter all quotes and paraphrased material from Mark Bula are based on my interview with Bula on April 4, 2018.

2. Big River Steel, *Big River Steel Opening Day: Dave Stickler Presentation*, video, 28:51 minutes, March 9, 2018, https://www.youtube.com/watch?v=HmNcku qdLtQ.

3. Abraham Maslow, *Motivation and Personality*, Harper & Row, New York, 1954.

4. Claudia Wallis, "The Science of Happiness," *Time*, February 25, 2005.

5. Claire Eagleton, Sarre Hayes, Abdrew Natthews, Gemma Perman, and Colette R. Hirscha, "The Power of Positive Thinking: Pathological Worry Is Reduced by Thought Replacement in Generalized Anxiety Disorder," *Behavior Research and Therapy*, vol. 78, 2016, pp. 13–18; and Jane E. Brody, "A Positive Outlook May Be Good for Your Health," *New York Times*, March 27, 2017, https://www.nytimes .com/2017/03/27/well/live/positive-thinking-may-improve-health-and-extend -life.html.

6. Teresa Amabile and Steven Kramer, *The Progress Principle: Using Small Wins to Ignite Joy, Engagement, and Creativity at Work*, Harvard Business Review Press, Boston, 2014.

7. Teresa Amabile and Steven Kramer, "The Power of Small Wins," *Harvard Business Review*, May 2011, https://hbr.org/2011/05/the-power-of-small-wins.

8. Mihaly Csikszentmihalyi, *Flow*, Harper Perennial, New York, 1990.

9. Kronos "Study Finds Employee Engagement Critical to Fixing the Financial Industry," https://www.kronos.com/about-us/newsroom/study-finds-employee -engagement-critical-fixing-financial-industry. Accessed May 30, 2018.

10. Unless otherwise noted, in this chapter all quotes and paraphrased comments from Chris Voss are from my interview with Voss on February 21, 2018. Voss also covers this subject matter in his book entitled *Never Split the Difference*, Harper-Collins, New York, 2016.

11. Edgar Zapata, "An Assessment of Cost Improvements in the NASA COTS/CRS Program and Implications for Future NASA Missions," paper presented at the American Institute of Aeronautics and Astronautics (AIAA) Space 2017 Conference, September 12, 2017, https://ntrs.nasa.gov/archive/nasa/casi.ntrs.nasa.gov/20170008895.pdf.

12. Michael Mankins and Eric Garton, *Time, Talent, Energy: Overcome Organizational Drag and Unleash Your Team's Productive Power*, Harvard Business Review Press, Boston, 2017; and Stephanie Vozza, "Why Employees at Apple and Google Are More Productive," *Fast Company*, March 13, 2017, https://www.fastcompany.com/3068771/how-employees-at-apple-and-google-are-more-productive.

13. Kathleen McCaffrey, "10 Genius Examples of How to Encourage Employee Innovation," *LHBS Collection*, February 17, 2017, https://medium.com/lhbs-collection/10-genius-examples-of-how-to-encourage-employee-innovation-8794d2bec5ad.

14. Simone Ahuja, "How Intuit Built a Better Support System for Intrapreneurs," *Harvard Business Review*, April 5, 2016, https://hbr.org/2016/04/how-intuit-built-a-better-support-system-for-intrapreneurs.

15. Julie Bort, "Jeff Bezos Explains the Perfect Way to Make Risky Business Decisions," *Business Insider*, April 12, 2017, https://www.businessinsider.com/jeff-bezos-explains-the-perfect-way-to-make-risky-business-decisions-2017-4.

16. Unless otherwise noted, in this chapter all quotes and paraphrased comments from James Citrin are from my interview with Citrin on March 7, 2018.

17. Jerry Sternin, "Practice Positive Deviance for Extraordinary Social Change," in Louis Carter, Roland Sullivan, Marshall Goldsmith, Dave Ulrich, and Norm Smallwood, editors, *The Change Champion's Field Guide: Strategies and Tools for Leading Change in Your Organization*, 2nd ed., Wiley, San Francisco, 2013, pp. 73–94.

18. Richard Pascale, Jerry Sternin, and Monique Sternin, *The Power of Positive Deviance: How Unlikely Innovators Solve the World's Toughest Problems*, Harvard Business Review Press, Boston, 2010.

19. David Dorsey, "Positive Deviant," *Fast Company*, November 30, 2000, https://www.fastcompany.com/42075/positive-devian.

20. Jane Lewis, "Positive Deviance: A Case Study in Finding and Harnessing the Wisdom of Organizational Communities," *Business Information Review*, vol. 26, no. 4, 2009, pp. 282–287, https://hiddeninsights.co.uk/wp-content/uploads/downloads/2011/04/JL-BIR-article.pdf.

21. Unless otherwise noted, in this chapter all quotes and paraphrased comments from Michael Arena are from my interview with Arena on February 14, 2018.

22. John Donovan and Cathy Benko, "AT&T's Talent Overhaul," *Harvard Business Review*, October 2016, https://hbr.org/2016/10/atts-talent-overhaul.

23. George, Bill. "The Leadership Quality that Truly Separates Disney's Bob Iger From His Peers," *Fortune*, April 4, 2016, http://fortune.com/2016/04/04/the -leadership-quality-that-truly-separates-disneys-bob-iger-from-his-peers/.

24. This quote is commonly attributed to Albert Einstein, but there's no clear evidence that these are his words.

25. Based on material provided to the author by WD-40 CEO Garry Ridge and Stan Sewitch, VP Global Organization Development, January 30, 2018.

26. Adam Bryant, "Jim Hackett on Authentic Leadership," *New York Times*, August 18, 2012, https://www.nytimes.com/2012/08/19/business/james-hackett-of -steelcase-on-authentic-leadership.html.

27. Based on material provided to the author by WD-40 CEO Garry Ridge.

28. Jordan Novet, "Intel CEO to Employees: 'We Are Going to Take More Risks,'" CNCB, December 19, 2017, https://www.cnbc.com/2017/12/19/intel-ceo-in -memo-we-are-going-to-take-more-risks.html.

29. Sylvia Ann Hewlett, Melinda Marshall, and Laura Sherbin, "How Diversity Can Drive Innovation," *Harvard Business Review*, December 2013, https://hbr .org/2013/12/how-diversity-can-drive-innovation.

30. Bryan Adams, "How Google's 20 Percent Rule Can Make You More Productive and Energetic," *Inc.*, December 28, 2016, https://www.inc.com/bryan-adams/12 -ways-to-encourage-more-free-thinking-and-innovation-into-any-business.html.

31. Charles A. O'Reilly and Michael L. Tushman, "The Ambidextrous Organization," *Harvard Business Review*, April 2004, https://hbr.org/2004/04/the-ambidextrous-organization; and Charles A. O'Reilly and Michael L. Tushman, *Lead and Disrupt: How to Solve the Innovator's Dilemma*, Stanford University Press, Stanford, 2016.

32. Kim Cameron, Carlos Mora, Trevor Leutscher, and Margaret Calarco, "Effects of Positive Practices on Organizational Effectiveness," *Journal of Applied Behavioral Science*, vol. 47, no. 3, 2011, pp. 266–308; and Sonja Lyubomirsky, Laura King, and Ed Diener, "The Benefits of Frequent Positive Affect: Does Happiness Lead to Success?" *Psychological Bulletin*, vol. 131, no. 6, 2005, pp. 803–855, https:// www.apa.org/pubs/journals/releases/bul-1316803.pdf.

33. Emma Seppälä, "Positive Teams Are More Productive," *Harvard Business Review*, March 18, 2015, https://hbr.org/2015/03/positive-teams-are-more-productive.

34. Marguerite Ward, "4 Reasons People Love Working at Southwest, Which Has Never Laid off a Single Employee," *CNBC Make It*, December 9, 2016, https:// www.cnbc.com/2016/12/09/4-reasons-people-love-working-at-southwest -which-has-never-laid-off-a-single-employee.html.

35. Thomas Sy, Stéphane Côté, and Richard Saavedra, "The Contagious Leader: Impact of the Leader's Mood on the Mood of Group Members, Group Affective Tone, and Group Processes," *Journal of Applied Psychology*, vol. 90, no. 2, 2005, pp. 295–305, http://psycnet.apa.org/record/2005-02538-007.

36. Shauna Carey, "A Lesson in Optimism," IDEO.org, June 2016, https://www .ideo.org/perspective/a-lesson-in-optimism.

Chapter 5

1. George Beall, "The Importance of Sticking to Your Company Values," *The Next Web*, October 17, 2017, https://thenextweb.com/contributors/2017/10/18/importance-sticking-company-values/.

2. Patagonia, "Patagonia's Mission Statement," last modified 2018, https://www.patagonia.com/company-info.html.

3. Anne Fisher, "How Patagonia Keeps Employee Turnover 'Freakishly Low,'" *Fortune*, June 9, 2016, http://fortune.com/2016/06/09/patagonia-employee-turnover/.

4. Todd Henneman, "Patagonia Fills Payroll with People Who Are Passionate," *Workforce*, November 5, 2011, http://www.workforce.com/2011/11/05/patagonia-fills-payroll-with-people-who-are-passionate/.

5. Unless otherwise noted, in this chapter, all quotes and paraphrased comments from Howard Behar are from my interview with Behar on November 7, 2018.

6. Jim Collins and Jerry Porras, *Built to Last: Successful Habits of Visionary Companies*, Harper Business, New York, 2004.

7. Patrick M. Lencioni, "Make Your Values Mean Something," *Harvard Business Review*, July 2002, https://hbr.org/2002/07/make-your-values-mean-something.

8. Patrick Wong, "Does More Money Change What We Value at Work?" *Glassdoor*, January 17, 2017, https://www.glassdoor.com/research/more-money-change-value-at-work/.

9. Ibid.

10. Punit Renjen, "Culture of Purpose: A Business Imperative," *2013 Core Beliefs & Culture Survey*, Deloitte, 2013, p. 4, https://www2.deloitte.com/content/dam/Deloitte/us/Documents/about-deloitte/us-leadership-2013-core-beliefs-culture-survey-051613.pdf.

11. Johnson & Johnson, "Our Credo," last modified 2018, https://www.jnj.com/about-jnj/jnj-credo.

12. Stephen A. Greyser, *Johnson & Johnson: The Tylenol Tragedy*, Harvard Business School Case 583-043, October 1982 (revised May 1992), https://www.hbs.edu/faculty/Pages/item.aspx?num=17858.

13. Nate Dvorak and Bailey Nelson, "Few Employees Believe in Their Company's Values," *Gallup Business Journal*, September 13, 2016, https://news.gallup.com/businessjournal/195491/few-employees-believe-company-values.aspx.

14. Halah Touryalai, "The Gospel According to Wells Fargo," *Forbes*, January 25, 2012, https://www.forbes.com/sites/halahtouryalai/2012/01/25/the-gospel-according-to-wells-fargo/#7ed8cce87904.

15. Digital Marketing Resource Center, *Leveraging Core Values for Competitive Advantage*, case study, http://dmresourcecenter.com/unit-5/core-values/. Accessed August 15, 2018.

16. Knowledge@Warton, "Tylenol and the Legacy of J&J's James Burke," *Leadership*, October 2, 2012, http://knowledge.wharton.upenn.edu/article/tylenol-and-the-legacy-of-jjs-james-burke/.

17. Unless otherwise noted, in this chapter all quotes and paraphrased comments from John Tu are from my interview with Tu on December 21, 2017.

18. Stuart Anderson, "Family Immigration Led to John Tu's Billion Dollar Company," *Forbes*, December 19, 2017, https://www.forbes.com/sites/stuartanderson /2017/12/19/family-immigration-led-to-john-tus-billion-dollar-company /#266995c65c1c.

19. Carol L. Cone, *5 Years of Purpose: The Reengineering of Brand Marketing*, executive summary, goodpurpose 2012, Edelman, 2012, https://bschool.nus.edu.sg/pdf /acsep/2012-Edelman-goodpurpose%C2%AE-Study.pdf.

20. Glassdoor, "Top HR Statistics: The Latest Stats for HR & Recruiting Pros," *Glassdoor for Employers*, last modified 2016, https://www.glassdoor.com/employers/popular -topics/hr-stats.htm.

21. Unless otherwise noted, in this chapter, all quotes and paraphrased comments from Jeanette Winters are from my interview with Winters on April 3, 2018.

22. Tony Hsieh, "How Zappos Infuses Culture Using Core Values," *Harvard Business Review*, May 24, 2010, https://hbr.org/2010/05/how-zappos-infuses-culture-using -core-values.

23. Unless otherwise noted, in this chapter, all quotes and paraphrased comments from Eric Fink are from my interview with Fink on September 8, 2017.

24. Alan Lewis, "How My Company Hires for Culture First, Skills Second," *Harvard Business Review*, January 26, 2011, https://hbr.org/2011/01/how-my-company -hires-for-cultu. Accessed August 15, 2018.

25. Unless otherwise noted, in this chapter all quotes and paraphrased comments from Tom Kolditz are from my interview with Kolditz on March 28, 2018.

26. Best Practice Instutite (BPI), "Novozymes Proves That Sustainability Pays," *UN Global Compact*, 2015, pp. 1–4, https://www.unglobalcompact.org/docs/issues _doc/lead/examples/Novozymes.pdf.

27. John Mackey, "Letter to Stakeholders," Whole Foods, https://www.wholefoodsmarket .com/sites/default/files/media/Global/Company%20Info/PDFs/ar07_letter.pdf.

28. Kermit Pattison, "Chip Conley Took the Maslow Pyramid, Made It an Employee Pyramid and Saved His Company," *Fast Cmpany*, August 26, 2010, https://www .fastcompany.com/1685009/chip-conley-took-maslow-pyramid-made-it -employee-pyramid-and-saved-his-company.

Chapter 6

1. Unless otherwise noted, this story in this chapter and any quotes and paraphrased material from Howard Behar are from my interview with Behar on October 27, 2017. The same story is recounted from the perspective of Howard Schultz in his book *Pour Your Heart Into It: How Starbucks Built a Company One Cup at a Time*, Hatchette Books, New York, 1999.

2. Tony Schwartz and Christine Porath, "The Power of Meeting Your Employees' Needs," *Harvard Business Review*, June 30, 2014, https://hbr.org/2014/06/the -power-of-meeting-your-employees-needs.

3. Society for Human Resource Management (SHRM), "Employee Job Satisfaction and Engagement: Optimizing Organizational Culture for Success," SHRM, 2014.

4. David Balovich, "Respect in the Workplace," *Creditworthy News*, August 17, 2006, http://www.creditworthy.com/3jm/articles/cw81706.html.

5. Howard S. Friedman and Stephanie Booth-Kewley, "Personality, Type A Behaviour, and Coronary Heart Disease: The Role of Emotional Expression," *Journal of Personality and Social Psychology*, vol. 53, no. 4, 1987, pp. 783–792.

6. Sally Kane, "Workplace Bullying Stories," *The Balance Careers*, June 11, 2018, https://www.thebalancecareers.com/bullying-stories-2164317.

7. American Psychological Association (APA) Center for Organizational Excellence, *Workplace Bullying*, video, 2:45 minutes, January 22, 2014, https://www.youtube.com/watch?v=-bhrqQ5zNmc.

8. David Rohde, "The Anti-Walmart: The Secret Sauce of Wegmans Is People," *Atlantic*, March 23, 2012, https://www.theatlantic.com/business/archive/2012/03/the-anti-walmart-the-secret-sauce-of-wegmans-is-people/254994/.

9. *Fortune*, "Fortune 100 Best 2017: Wegmans Food Markets," http://fortune.com/best-companies/wegmans-food-markets/.

10. Pamela N. Danziger, "Why Wegmans Food Markets Gets the Love of Customers," *Forbes*, March 3, 2018, https://www.forbes.com/sites/pamdanziger/2018/03/03/why-wegmans-food-markets-gets-the-love-of-customers/2/#6590283357b7.

11. Mark Feffer, "What Makes an Employer a Great Place to Work? It Takes Conscious Effort to Build and Maintain a Workplace Where Every Employee Feels Like a Star," Society for Human Resource Management (SHRM), June 1, 2015, https://www.shrm.org/hr-today/news/hr-magazine/pages/0615-great-places-to-work.aspx.

12. Ibid.

13. Michael Hess, "Could This Be the Best Company in the World?" *CBS MoneyWatch*, September 13, 2011, https://www.cbsnews.com/news/could-this-be-the-best-company-in-the-world/.

14. Market Force, "New Market Force Information Study Finds Publix and Wegmans Are America's Favorite Grocery Stores," *Market Force Information*, May 9, 2017, https://www.marketforce.com/2017-market-research-on-americas-favorite-grocery-chains.

15. David Rohde, "The Anti-Walmart."

16. Paul J. Zak, "The Neuroscience of Trust," *Harvard Business Review*, January 2017, https://hbr.org/2017/01/the-neuroscience-of-trust.

17. Vivian Hunt, Dennis Layton, and Sara Prince, "Why Diversity Matters," *McKinsey & Company*, January 2015, https://www.mckinsey.com/business-functions/organization/our-insights/why-diversity-matters.

18. Josh Bersin, "Why Diversity and Inclusion Has Become a Business Priority," *Josh Bersin*, last modified May 9, 2016, https://joshbersin.com/2015/12/why-diversity-and-inclusion-will-be-a-top-priority-for-2016/.

19. Jeff Kauflin, "America's Best Employers for Diversity," *Forbes*, January 23, 2018, https://www.forbes.com/sites/jeffkauflin/2018/01/23/americas-best-employers -for-diversity/#3023d9047164.

20. Mike Stallard, "3 Practices CEOs Can Learn from the Girl Scouts," *Connection Culture Group*, February 5, 2014, http://connectionculture.com/post/3-practices -ceos-can-learn-girl-scouts.

21. Unless otherwise noted, in this chapter all quotes and paraphrased material from Frances Hesselbein are from my interview with Hesselbein on September 16, 2015.

22. Paolo Gaudiano and Ellen Hunt, "Diversity from the Bottom Up: Lessons and Insights from Tech Leader Atlassian," *Forbes*, March 27, 2017, https://www .forbes.com/sites/gaudianohunt/2017/03/27/atlassian-diversity-reports/#40730 bb45a43.

23. Unless otherwise noted, in this chapter all quotes and paraphrased material from Dominic Barton are from my interview with Barton on November 26, 2017.

24. Paolo Gaudiano and Ellen Hunt, "Diversity from the Bottom Up."

25. Christine Porath, "The Leadership Behavior That's Most Important to Employees," *Harvard Business Review*, May 11, 2015, https://hbr.org/2015/05/the-leadership -behavior-thats-most-important-to-employees.

26. Daniel Goleman, *Emotional Intelligence*, Bantam Books, New York, 1995.

27. Flaum, "When It Comes to Business Leadership, Nice Guys Finish First: A Green Peak Partners Study Shows That Conventional Wisdom Is Wrong—and That Leaders Who Possess Strong Soft Skills Perform Better at Driving Hard Results," *Green Peak Partners*, https://greenpeakpartners.com/wp-content/uploads /2018/09/Green-Peak_Cornell-University-Study_What-predicts-success.pdf.

28. "How CEO Garry Ridge Has Made WD-40 a Well-Oiled Machine," *Simply Communicate*, February 6, 2016, https://simply-communicate.com/ceo-garry -ridge-made-wd-40-well-oiled-machine/.

29. Ibid.

30. Dr. Terry Jackson is a trusted advisor and coach to C-suite executives. He is the author of *Transformational Thinking: The First Toward Personal and Organizational Greatness*, Amazon Digital Services, and the COO of JCG Consulting Group. The quotes and this story came to me from Jackson directly.

31. Glassdoor Survey, "Employers to Retain Half of Their Employees Longer If Bosses Showed More Appreciation," *Glassdoor for Employers*, November 13, 2013, https://www.glassdoor.com/employers/blog/employers-to-retain-half-of-their -employees-longer-if-bosses-showed-more-appreciation-glassdoor-survey/.

32. Christine Porath and Douglas R. Conant, "The Key to Campbell Soup's Turn-around? Civility," *Harvard Business Review*, October 5, 2017, https://hbr.org/2017 /10/the-key-to-campbell-soups-turnaround-civility.

33. Elisa Boxer, "Home Depot's CEO Did This 25,000 Times. Science Says You Should Do It Too," *Inc.*, November 10, 2017, https://www.inc.com/elisa-boxer/home -depots-ceo-did-this-25000-times-science-says-you-should-do-it-too.html.

Chapter 7

1. Todd Spangler, "Netflix Booms in Q1 to Hit 125 Million Streaming Subscribers, Again Beating Forecasts," *Variety*, April 16, 2018, https://variety.com/2018/digital/news/netflix-q1-2018-earnings-beat-expectations-1202754386/.

2. James Ledbetter, "America's Most Underestimated Company," *Slate*, September 1, 2010, http://www.slate.com/articles/business/moneybox/2010/09/americas_most_underestimated_company.html.

3. Kevin Kruse, "Netflix Culture Deck Co-Creator Says Leaders Need to Explain Context," *Forbes*, February 19, 2018, https://www.forbes.com/sites/kevinkruse/2018/02/19/netflix-culture-deck-co-creator-says-leaders-need-to-explain-context/#4d6e4097590c.

4. Reed Hastings, "Actual Company Values—Culture," SlideShare, August 1, 2009, https://www.slideshare.net/reed2001/culture-1798664/8-Actual_company_values_are_thebehaviors.

5. Nancy Hass, "And the Award for the Next HBO Goes to . . . ," *GQ*, January 29, 2013, https://www.gq.com/story/netflix-founder-reed-hastings-house-of-cards-arrested-development?mobify=0.

6. Ibid.

7. Bobby Medlin and Kenneth W. Green, Jr., "Enhancing Performance Through Goal Setting, Engagement, and Optimism," *Industrial Management & Data Systems*, vol. 109, no. 7, 2009, pp. 943–956, https://doi.org/10.1108/02635570910982292.

8. Hannah J. P. Klug and Günter W. Maie, "Linking Goal Progress and Subjective Well-Being: A Meta-analysis," *Journal of Happiness Studies*, vol. 16, no. 1, 2015, pp. 37–65, https://doi.org/10.1007/s10902-013-9493-0.

9. Dan Ariely, *What Makes Us Feel Good About Our Work?* TED channel, video, 20:26 minutes, April 10, 2013, https://www.youtube.com/watch?v=5aH2Ppjpcho&itct=CBIQpDAYACITCOugx8ja5tcCFUvPAwod6kAP3zIHcmVsYXRlZEiHuKyRhb2ombUB&app=desktop.

10. Teresa Amabile and Steven J. Kramer, "The Power of Small Wins," *Harvard Business Review*, May 2011, https://hbr.org/2011/05/the-power-of-small-wins.

11. Lisa Evans, "Why Sharing Your Progress Makes You More Likely to Accomplish Your Goals," *Fast Company*, June 19, 2015, https://www.fastcompany.com/3047432/why-sharing-your-progress-makes-you-more-likely-to-accomplish-your-goals.

12. Andrew J. Oswald, Eugenio Proto, and Daniel Sgroi, "Happiness and Productivity," *Journal of Labor Economics*, vol. 33, no. 4, 2015, pp. 789–822, http://wrap.warwick.ac.uk/63228/.

13. Best Practice Institute, BPI Nurses Survey, http://www.bestpracticeboard.com/nursesurvey.htm. Accessed August 15, 2018.

14. Sim B. Sitkin, C. Chet Miller, and Kelly E. See, "The Stretch Goal Paradox," *Harvard Business Review*, January 2017, https://hbr.org/2017/01/the-stretch-goal-paradox.

15. Unless otherwise noted, in this chapter all quotes and paraphrased material attributed to James Citrin are from my interview with Citrin on March 7, 2018.

16. Kavita Kumar, "Best Buy Moves from Renew Blue Turnaround to Growth Phase." *Star Tribune*, March 4, 2017, http://www.startribune.com/best-buy-moves-from -renew-blue-turnaround-to-growth-phase/415357004/.

17. Bill Taylor, "How WD-40 Created a Learning-Obsessed Company Culture," *Harvard Business Review*, September 16, 2016, https://hbr.org/2016/09/how-wd -40-created-a-learning-obsessed-company-culture.

18. Best Buy, *Renew Blue*, November 12, 2012, p. 28, https://corporate.bestbuy.com /wp-content/uploads/BestBuy_Web_FINAL.pdf.

19. Unless otherwise noted, in this chapter all quotes and paraphrased material attrib- uted to Tom Kolditz are from my interview with Kolditz on March 28, 2018.

20. Kris Duggan, "Six Companies That Are Redefining Performance Management," *Fast Company*, December 15, 2015, https://www.fastcompany.com/3054547/six -companies-that-are-redefining-performance-management.

21. John Doerr, "When John Doerr Brought a 'Gift' to Google's Founders," *Wired*, April 24, 2018, https://www.wired.com/story/when-john-doerr-brought-a-gift -to-googles-founders/; and John Doerr, *Measure What Matters*, Portfolio Penguin, New York, 2018.

22. Josh Bersin, "Becoming Irresistible: A New Model for Employee Engagement," *Deloitte Insights*, January 26, 2015, https://www2.deloitte.com/insights/us/en /deloitte-review/issue-16/employee-engagement-strategies.html#endnote-44.

23. Eric Fink of Jazz Pharmaceuticals, interview with the author on September 8. 2017.

24. Visa, "Client Story: Visa University," *Watershed*, https://www.watershedlrs.com /visa-university-client-story.

25. John Donovan and Cathy Benko, "AT&T's Talent Overhaul," *Harvard Business Review*, October 2016, https://hbr.org/2016/10/atts-talent-overhaul.

26. Ritz-Carlton, "The Upside of Daily Line-up," *Ritz-Carlton Leadership Center* blog, December 3, 2014, http://ritzcarltonleadershipcenter.com/2014/12/upside -daily-line-up/.

27. "Cheesecake Factory Cooks up a Rigorous Employee Training Program," South- Western, last modified 2006, http://www.swlearning.com/management/hrm _news/training_0706_01.html.

28. Nicci Strong, "'Gamifying' Training [with the Cheesecake Factory]," *EnGaming*, June 15, 2012, https://engaming.wordpress.com/2012/06/15/gamifying-training -with-the-cheesecake-factory/.

29. Unless otherwise noted, in this chapter all quotes and paraphrased material attrib- uted to Admiral Mark T. Guadagnini are from my interview with Admiral Gua- dagnini on May 8, 2013.

30. Carol S. Dweck, *Mindset: The New Psychology of Success*, Ballantine, New York, 2006.

31. Sarah Bond and Dr. Gillian Shapiro, *Touch at the Top? New Rule for Resilience for Women's Leadership Success*, Business Sake Consulting Ltd & Shapiro Consulting Ltd., 2014, https://forbusinessake.files.wordpress.com/2014/11/tough_at_the _top.pdf.

32. American Management Association (AMA), *Agility and Resilience in the Face of Continuous Change*, AMA, last modified 2006, https://www.amanet.org/images /hri-agility06.pdf.

33. David Kiger, "Resilience Is Essential for Long-Term CEO Success," Business 2 Community, April 3, 2017, https://www.business2community.com/leadership /resilience-essential-long-term-ceo-success-01811657.

34. Susan Sorenson, "How Employees' Strengths Make Your Company Stronger," Gallup, February 20, 2014, https://news.gallup.com/businessjournal/167462 /employees-strengths-company-stronger.aspx.

35. Jim Asplund, James K. Harter, Sangeeta Agrawal, and Stephanie K. Plowman, "The Relationship Between Strength-Based Employee Development and Organizational Outcomes," Gallup, July 2016, https://static1.squarespace.com /static/577a17d9d482e9e2bce9bc68/t/58d4e81a20099e1b037cbced/1490348 060515/2015+Relationship+between+Strengths-based+employee+development +and+organizational+outcomes+-+Gallup+StrengthsFinder+Singapore.pdf.

36. Henry Stewart, "8 Companies That Celebrate Mistakes," LinkedIn, June 8, 2015, https://www.linkedin.com/pulse/8-companies-celebrate-mistakes-henry -stewart/.

37. Richard Branson, "You Learn by Doing and by Falling Over," Virgin, October 27, 2014, https://www.virgin.com/richard-branson/you-learn-doing-and-falling -over.

38. Andrew P. Hill and Thomas Curran, "Multidimensional Perfectionism and Burnout: A Meta-Analysis," *Personality and Social Psychology Review*, vol. 20, no. 3, 2015, pp. 269–288, http://journals.sagepub.com/doi/abs/10.1177/1088868315596286.

39. "The Employee Burnout Crisis: Study Reveals Big Workplace Challenge in 2017," Kronos Incorporated, January 9, 2017, https://www.kronos.com/about-us /newsroom/employee-burnout-crisis-study-reveals-big-workplace-challenge-2017.

40. Fawn Johnson, "These Companies Know How to Treat Employees Right," *Atlantic*, December 9, 2014, https://www.theatlantic.com/business/archive/2014/12 /these-companies-know-how-to-treat-employees-right/425868/.

Chapter 8

1. Marshall Goldsmith and Sal Silvester, "Stakeholder Centered Coaching Model," *Stakeholder Centered Coaching: Maximizing Your Impact as a Coach*, THiNKaha, Cupertino, CA, 2018.

INDEX

ABOUT THE AUTHOR

 **Louis Carter** is an organizational psychologist and one of the top executive coaches to C-level executives of major companies such as Kimberly-Clark, the Federal Reserve Bank of New York, Saudi Aramco, Duke Energy, Shire, Jazz Pharmaceuticals, KeyBank, J&J, Madison Square Garden, TIAA (formerly TIAA-CREF), and many more. He has helped them transform themselves and transform their organizations into environments their employees love and in which their employees want to produce the best results for their company.

He is the author of over 10 books on best practices in leadership development and talent management including *The Change Champion's Field Guide, Best Practices in Leadership Development and Organization Change,* and *Best Practices in Talent Management.* He is a proud member of the MG 100 Coaches project, chosen from over 12,000 coaches by his longtime mentor Marshall Goldsmith. Louis is the recipient of *Elearning! Magazine'*s Trailblazer Award and HR Tech Conference's Top Products Award. He has also been included in *Leadership Excellence* magazine's Best in Leadership Development for his work as founder and CEO of Best Practice Institute and as the creator of the first anytime 360-degree feedback tool based on feedforward and appreciative dialogue: the Skillrater Anytime Feedback tool.

Louis Carter founded Best Practice Institute in 2001 while obtaining his graduate degree from Columbia University. He facilitated drum circles in New York City after the 9/11 attacks to help rebuild the community. He further developed this concept into the BPI Senior Executive Board, a benchmark research consortium comprising C-level executives from Fortune 500 companies who want to transform themselves and their organizations through best practices in leadership and organization development.

He has spoken for the prime minister of the United Arab Emirates' HR Lighthouse Initiative. He has also spoken to Pentagon and UN officials and to various international conferences on his work and research. He has been a drummer for over five bands throughout the past 30 years, and he volunteers to drum for community drum circles and children's centers.